Inner Growth / Outer Change

John H. Westerhoff, III

INNER
GROWTH
OUTER
CHANGE

*An Educational Guide
to Church Renewal*

A Crossroad Book
The Seabury Press • New York

Second printing

1979 / The Seabury Press
815 Second Avenue / New York, N.Y. 10017

Printed in the United States of America

Library of Congress Cataloging in Publication Data
Westerhoff, John H   Inner growth, outer change.
1. Church renewal. I. Title.
BV600.2.W49   262'.001   79-4359   ISBN 0-8164-2213-3

Grateful acknowledgment is made to the following individuals and publishers for permission to use the materials listed:

The Ecumenical Women's Centers—for the following hymns as revised and published in *Because We Are One People: Songs for Worship*, copyright 1974: "Dear Mother-Father of Us All"; "Blest Be the Tie That Binds"; "For All the Saints"; "Immortal, Invisible, God Only Wise"; "O God, Our Help in Ages Past"; "Now Thank We All Our God"; "God Rest You Joyful People All"; "Lead on, O Cloud of Yahweh," by Ruth Duck © 1974.

The Editor's Literary Estate and Chatto & Windus Ltd.—for "A Prayer" (Be Thou My Vision) from *The Poem Book of the Gael*, selected and edited by Eleanor Hull.

Roger W. Holmes—for the hymn "The Voice of God Is Calling" by John Haynes Holmes.

Theo Oxenham—for the hymn "In Christ There Is No East or West" by John Oxenham.

Arthur I. Waskow and Holt, Rinehart and Winston, Inc.—for material in "The Seder" from *The Freedom Seder: A New Haggadah for Passover* by Arthur I. Waskow, copyright © 1969, 1970 by The Religious Community of Micah.

Contents

Preface

This book has been writing itself for some time. It marks a turning point in my own pilgrimage. In one way or another, as long as I can remember, I have been concerned, on the one hand, with religious experience, piety, and the Catholic substance of our faith, and on the other hand with prophetic witness, politics, and the Protestant principle of critical judgment. In *Tomorrow's Church* I struggled with an aspect of this concern. In *Will Our Children Have Faith?* and my new book, *Learning Through Liturgy*, I have explored other dimensions. *Inner Growth / Outer Change* focuses on the connection between *Piety and Politics*. It is one more small piece in my continuing effort to search for a catechesis that will nurture religious experience and political action, that will be faithful to both Catholic substance and Protestant principle.

I do not think that I have achieved my goal, but perhaps together we can take a step forward. Like *Values for Tomorrow's Children* this book is intended to be *our* book. I hope that you will write in the margins, change and correct the text, engage in the exercises at the beginning of each chapter, and reconceive the educational experiences suggested in the last section of the book. I do not believe I have the answers; indeed I keep changing my mind. But I do hope I can stimulate you to think for yourself and to come to some decisions that you are willing to live—and perhaps die—for.

One more comment that may help you to understand aspects of this book: After 20 meaningful years of Christian fellowship and faithful service as a minister in the United Church of Christ, and after a number of years of prayer and reflection, I made the difficult decision to become an Episcopal priest. The United Church of Christ and the three parishes I served nurtured me and my family in Christian faith and the Protestant prophetic spirit. I am grateful. Within the unity of Christ's church, there are various expressions that witness to the truth of the Gospel we all share. But my longing for the Catholic side of the faith and my need to mediate between Catholic and Protestant led me to the Episcopal Church. I am appreciative for the past and joyfully hopeful about the future. May we one day all be one.

I understand myself first of all as a parish priest; as such I am engaged in the formation of spiritual leaders for the church. My primary concerns are focused on pastoral theology (or divinity) and the integration of catechesis (education), liturgics (worship), and the care and nurturing of souls (counseling). My work takes me to parishes across this continent, where I find my roots and inspiration. However, I struggle daily with my own spiritual life of prayer and witness. This book is a testimony to my pilgrimage and strivings—a small gift to Catholic and Protestant friends who share faith in the Gospel. May it be an ecumenical resource in our shared continuing quest for a reformed church, a renewed faith, and a faithful educational ministry.

I would like to express gratitude to my secretary, Mrs. Lesta Gotsch, who typed this manuscript; to Dieter Hessel, who encouraged me to write this book and helped in many ways to improve it; to my students and colleagues at Duke, who have stimulated me to look at new questions and seek new answers; to lay persons and clergy across the land who have inspired me by their faithfulness; and most important, to my wife, Barnie, and our children, Jill, Jack, and Beth, who have supported me through my pilgrimage, affirmed my decisions, and given me the reasons to continue seeking a catechesis for the future. I only hope and pray that my labors—labors which have kept me from being fully the husband and father I have always wanted to be—have not prevented me from witnessing with them to the Christian faith, mission, and ministry to which I have committed my life.

Pentecost 1978   *Duke University Divinity School*

Introduction
Dieter T. Hessel

This book emerged from the interaction of pastors, consultants, and national staff of several denominations who met to explore how to foster whole Christian communities. In a time of reaction against corporate social action, and a resurgence of individualistic, legalistic piety, church leaders need to cultivate healthy approaches to both inner growth and outer change. A faithful church will redevelop these complementary aspects of Christian faith in an integrated way.

Whole congregations are able to unite religious experience with prophetic action. They exhibit both deep piety and courageous politics. A faithful church does not choose between personal contemplation and social witness; it is closer to God *and* to human need. As John Westerhoff puts it, "Piety without politics is barren, while politics without piety is soulless." For his exemplary model he chooses a sixteenth-century saint, Teresa of Ávila.

I wanted Westerhoff to write this manuscript because his theory and methods call for our immersion in an ecumenical, theological-liturgical tradition. Many of us have only a vague awareness of historic Christian disciplines. No wonder some of our people have "turned east" or "turned right" in quest of spiritual renewal. But authentic spirituality depends on living that is more directly related to the words and deeds of Jesus than are the techniques of Yoga, Buddhism, Hinduism, or humanistic psychologies of prayer. Christian spirituality will also be more active for social justice than are popular neoevangelical groups or the electronic revivalists on those UHF channels.

Seekers of a new way, both in and outside the church, ought to be rebelling against shallow piety, perfunctory prayer, or privatistic

meditation. Can they, and we, be led to authentic prayer that is
centered in prophecy rather than in privatism, that is ethically serious rather than merely euphoric, and that is more empowering than
reassuring? Sören Kierkegaard once asserted that it is better to pray
to a wooden idol than to go through the motions with God. Mum-
bling hymns and prayers in church probably is worse than experi-
menting with non-Christian meditation or authoritarian sects. But
neither is desirable. Bad religion remains worse than none, because
it inoculates against faithfulness.

To foster fullness of Christian faith and community, we must become more discriminating about our liturgy—the content of both
worship and work. We will favor forms of worship that express concern for social justice. We will affirm with Westerhoff that prayer is a
way of life, a daily relationship with the God who acts in history.
"Only prayerfulness, a radical love of God and neighbor, is fully
satisfying. Serving God, seeking justice, is true prayer. Prayer implies an engagement with the world, a wrestling with the principalities and powers. Prayer is never an escape from the world or its
trials and tribulations."

The other church work that accompanies prayer will be worldly—
identifying with the suffering, advocating the rights and needs of the
oppressed, striving to release creative political, economic, and ad-
ministrative power toward the ends of the community of the New
Age. This book only begins to identify criteria for personal morality
and public policy that arise in the context of Christian faithfulness.
But it underscores the need for moral-political discourse and action
by those who would be spiritually alive. And it reminds us that the
Bible, when studied by people who are socially engaged, is the basic
resource for discernment and decision.

Part Two of *Inner Growth / Outer Change* presents the author's
educational philosophy. Westerhoff reviews dimensions of the
ministry of the Word, emphasizing social responsibility and lay participation. He outlines a common ministry concerned with reviving
vision, developing biblical understanding, experiencing and embodying the Word in all aspects of church program. He concludes
this section with a redefinition of Christian education as catechesis.
Westerhoff prefers "catechesis" to its synonym, "nurture," because
the term, though awkward, has a more historic and catholic and a less

placid or individualistic connotation. Catechesis refers dynamically to the church teaching by its life, to the members learning by participation in mission, to faith being caught more than taught. The basic educational question is: How shall we become communities of Christians in the world? The author suggests ways to interiorize the tradition, and thus re-formed, to respond to current issues.

Part Three, "Pathways to Faithfulness," is a flexible learning design, or a collection of designs presented as a 13-session model for catechesis. The learning method is consistent with current modes of action/reflection, including the AAAR (Awareness-Analysis-Action-Reflection) cycle of "Doing the Word," one of the Shared Approaches to Christian Education. The collection of designs suggests several configurations. Leaders are responsible for careful adaptation and use.

In an era of diverse approaches to church renewal, leaders of congregations and judicatories should scrutinize the assumptions and methods underlying any approach. They should also beware of acquiring a "bag of tricks" without attending to their underlying purpose. Try not to isolate elements of Westerhoff's learning design from the integrated theological framework of Part One and the educational philosophy of Part Two. Readers who skip over theory to acquire a few tools can hardly contribute to revitalized congregational life.

Even though there is no shortcut, there is no shortage of programs that offer cheap renewal (parallel to Bonhoeffer's "cheap" grace). The search for approaches that "go down easy" exposes a double irony: (1) A church undergoing a faith crisis cannot make itself faithful. Try as it will, the church cannot renew itself. But it can listen to the Word and respond to the faithfulness of God in the world. (2) Precisely at the decisive point, however, the church tends to fall back into privatized piety and to avoid new social responsibilities or costly social witness on the grounds that the church must do less to become more "spiritual." But the church has not been overly involved in working for humane social change; it only thinks it has. Meanwhile the turn inward only increases bad faith while it artificially prolongs certain institutional patterns.

Church renewal is based on authentic faith, which is God's gracious gift to the people who accept the invitation to participate in the New Age. The invitation is costly, requiring repentance. The path of transformation, as always, is christological. Any church that would save its current way of life will lose it. The community of faith, called to follow Jesus the Christ, will become quite different: "Adapt yourselves no longer to the pattern of the present world, but let your minds be remade and your whole nature thus transformed. Then you will be able to discern the will of God" (Romans 12:2 NEB).

Part One

FOUNDATIONS FOR FAITHFULNESS

Chapter 1

Reform and Renewal

The church is the family of God, a visible, historical, human community called to nurture its people in the Gospel tradition so that they might live under the judgment and inspiration of that tradition to the end that God's will is done and God's community comes. The church is the body of Christ, a hidden, prophetic creature of God's spirit, an instrument of God's transforming power, and a witness to God's continuing revelation in history.

It is one church, a paradox to the mind: sinful, yet holy; divided, yet one; continuously in need of reform, yet the bearer of God's transforming eternal Word; a human institution and a holy community; a disparate assembly of baptized sinners living, sometimes unconsciously, by grace, but also an intentional, obedient, steadfast, faithful company of converted, visible saints; a mystery even to its members, who are aware, nevertheless, in often incomprehensible ways, that the church has a mission in the world and a ministry to those who by birth or decision find themselves, not entirely by choice, within that family which bears the name Christian.

Today you and I find ourselves living within some poor expressions of this one, holy, catholic, and apostolic church. It can be confusing and trying. There are moments when the church seems to be among the most bankrupt, hopeless, of institutions. And yet there are other times when we are aware that the meaning and purpose of life is dependent upon this fragile community of faith and doubt, of faithfulness and faithlessness. The history of the church seems to be a story of great truths revealed and lost, heights of faith realized and forgotten, prophetic actions demonstrated and denied.

Today as in days past our common life and witness in the church is mixed. Yet there are signs of hope. Among Christian churches— Protestant, Roman, Orthodox—there is a worldwide movement toward mutual recognition and collaboration. Christians and Jews have made a first step toward reconciliation. Attitudes toward the world's other faith communities are more positive and respectful. Reform in the liturgy is reuniting separated sisters and brothers and transforming congregations. Popular piety and civil religion no longer are accepted uncritically. Christians and the churches are increasingly alert to the pressing social problems of the day. New understandings have emerged from these critical judgments the church has brought against itself. Here and there, new spirit has erupted among the faithful and the ministry of the laity has come into its own.

But that is not the whole picture. There are signs of despair. Tensions between the generations, the sexes, the races continue. Tremendous upheavals in the world and the emergence of new moral dilemmas leave many troubled and adrift. Change within and without the church has caused disorientation, confusion, and estrangement. New splits have occurred. Spirituality—the experience of life with God—has for many reached a new low. Growing economic trials and tribulations and a lack of spiritual leadership confound the church. Anti-intellectualism increases. Fewer persons attend the rituals of the church. Among many persons throughout the world the church has lost its credibility. Decisions on political, social, and economic life divide the church. And a new pietism has surfaced to insulate the church from the world.

People are confused. They lack a sense of corporate identity. They are without an agreed upon authority to which they can appeal and debate their differences. For some, the church is best understood in terms of doctrine in which the Scriptures and tradition are normative. Their primary concern is that all Christians assent to right belief. For others, the church is best understood in terms of religious experience in which the presence of the Holy Spirit and its gifts are normative. Their primary concern is that all Christians unite in prayer, fellowship, and an openness to the Spirit. For still others, the church is best understood as a social institution, either supporting personal needs or engaging in corporate service and action on behalf of humane causes in the society. Their primary concern is that the church serve human needs. The integration of these three understandings might appear easy in theory, but proves in practice to be extremely difficult.

Secular journalists, observing the confused self-image of the church and its mixed manifestations ask, as did the editors of *Newsweek:* "Has the Church Lost Her Soul?" It is an interesting question. But the answer, of course, is an unequivocal no! The soul of the church is not to be found in doctrine, in religious experience, or in outward forms or manifestations. The soul of the church is Jesus Christ. We cannot domesticate this Jesus in the church by our dogmatic affirmations, by our ecclesiastical systems, or by our lives of subjective individualism. We cannot base Christian faith on a wave of religious emotion, philosophical doctrine, or organizational development. Nor will we be helped by those who wish to embrace uncritically modern psychology or some other social science. A false modernity is no answer.

We can't ignore the obvious: There simply is no Christianity without Christ. To be Christian the church must affirm Jesus Christ as Lord. Christianity does not exist merely wherever humanity is realized. Humanity is realized outside Christianity. A Christian church is not any group of persons who strive to live a decent life in order to gain salvation. That too can be found outside the church. A Christian is not just any person of faith and good will. Only someone for whom the life, death, and resurrection of Jesus Christ is ultimately decisive may be called a Christian. Only a human community of which the same can be said may be called a church. Christianity only exists where the memory of this Christ is alive and his presence made real day by day in the being—the thought, feeling, and action—of persons and their community of faith.

But it isn't enough that we sing or say that Jesus Christ is Lord. We need to be clear about which Jesus we have made decisive in our lives, which Jesus we have made the authority for our faith. For the Christian, it is the Jesus of history; the Jesus with a simple and clear message: There is one God who acts in history and has an intention for creation, namely a world of peace, justice, unity, equity, and the health and well being of all. Jesus further proclaimed the coming of God's community. He announced that God's cause will, in spite of contrary evidence, prevail; that the future belongs to God. This same Jesus proclaimed one supreme norm for all human life: God's will, which was not a law or laws, but a way of being faithful. God's will, when it is done, will realize God's intentions for creation. Jesus,

therefore, was biased toward those who were denied God's intentions, but he identified himself with all people and their needs. He
acted on behalf of the sick, weak, lame, hurt, and oppressed. But he
also sought out the heretics, the hypocrites, and the immoral, bringing them both judgment and mercy and thereby converting them to
newness of life.

All this was good news and an example of life lived in unity with
God and God's will. Still he was killed. But God did not permit his
death to end his life. So it was that the little community who followed
him and called him Rabbi experienced amidst their doubt that the
crucified is living, that his death was dying into God. Jesus, the one
seemingly forsaken by God, lives with, through, and in God. Thus is
the cross an event of salvation and the resurrection a witness to God's
transforming power. Only then was the church formed. Jesus is the
Christ, God's Word (action) in history. And the church is the community of persons who profess in word and deed their faith in Jesus
Christ. We Christians bear his name, are set apart through baptism
in his name, sustained by his spirit so as to keep alive his memory
and vision, and united at his family meal so as to know his presence
and to be empowered by his grace. Christ is the soul of the church.

What does this mean for the church? It means that the church must
ever be Catholic in substance and Protestant in spirit. In Jesus Christ
the universal, eternal authority for Christian faith and life is given
and the tradition shaped. Continuity with the Word of God in Jesus
Christ must be protected and maintained. Still, because this divine
Word is held in human vessels, a prophetic judgment upon and
continual reform of our words and deeds are essential to the church's
life. We who affirm our faith in Jesus Christ owe a radical obedience
to God's coming community and are accountable to God's will. So it
is that we must always be reforming and renewing our faith and
commitment, our words and deeds, our common life and mission.

A renewed concentration on Jesus Christ will provide us with a
common ground for judging and inspiring our lives. Together we can
reform our limited and particular understandings and ways. We
need to defend the responsibility of preserving and communicating
the faith while not neglecting our responsibility continually to
examine it afresh and correct our ways in the light of our new understandings. Thereby will we be faithful. Church renewal and reform

are essential to faithful life. A church that is faithful to Jesus Christ
will be closer to God and at the same time closer to humanity; in
uniting religious experience with prophetic action the church becomes more Christian.

Chapter 2

A Christian Church

How do you envision Jesus Christ? The symbols we choose to represent our Lord both express and determine our understanding of the Christian life. Figure 2.1 is a triptych. In the three spaces provided draw, sketch, or describe in words the images or representations of Jesus that are most important to you (for example, the birth of Jesus or Jesus and the children). Next, on the lines under the triptych copy a verse from the Bible that best represents your understanding of the Christian church. Then write a paraphrase of this scriptural passage using as few of the original words as possible.

In Figure 2.2 you will find my responses to the exercise you just completed. It is not intended to be the correct answer against which you are to evaluate your own. It is meant to provide a context for our attempt to understand the nature of the Christian life, individual and corporate.

Our images of the Christian life and the Christian church keep changing. The times in which we live and our limited personal experiences significantly affect our understandings. Our understandings continually need to be reexamined. Our images need always to be reforming.

This century alone has witnessed the shift from one emphasis to another. Early in the century the church emphasized piety and the salvation of individual souls. Personal religious experience was central. This preoccupation resulted in a divorce of faithfulness from worldly life. Then came the era of the Social Gospel. The church rejected a marriage between church and society, but did not withdraw from the social world. An emphasis on prophetic witness and action followed. But the church became disenchanted with complex social policy issues. A new emphasis on personal piety emerged. By the Fifties that piety had accommodated to the culture and assumed

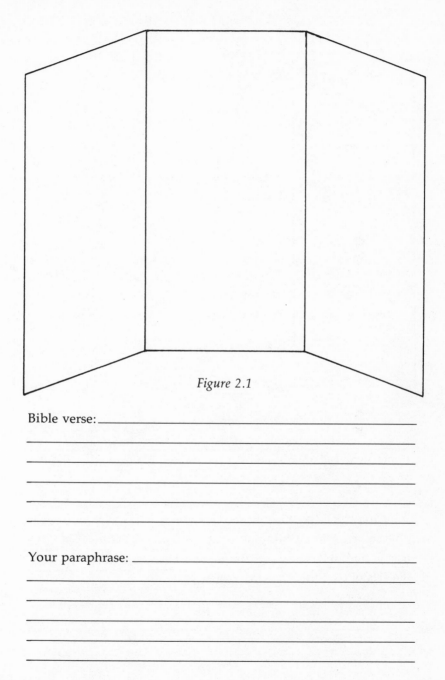

Figure 2.1

Bible verse:_____

_____

_____

_____

_____

_____

Your paraphrase: _____

_____

_____

_____

_____

_____

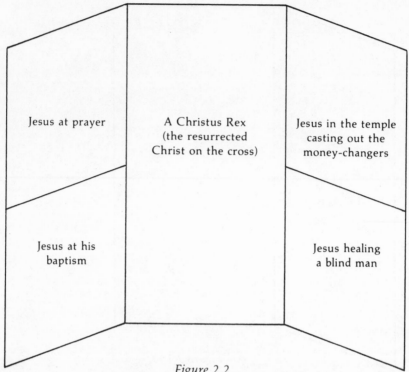

Figure 2.2

Bible verse: "But you are a chosen race, a royal priesthood, a holy nation, God's own people, that you may declare the wonderful deeds of him who called you out of darkness into his marvelous light" (1 Peter 2:9).

My paraphrase: We have been blessed and called to the awesome, undeserved responsibility of living so close to God that we might receive light and power, and through our deeds and words witness to the acts of God that transform all of life.

* * *

the shape of churchly life. The Sixties witnessed an alienation among many, though not most, of those who claimed the name of Christ. The alienated, with vigor and devotion, responded once again to a call for social action. The movements for civil rights, peace, and equality helped some in the church to rediscover the world. Prophetic action once again took the place of piety. And now in the Seventies, an awareness of society's deep sickness, the complexity of social issues, and the difficulty of judging what a Christian ought to do has in combination with typical American individualism caused the vast majority of church folk to opt for piety over politics. Once again we see a reassertion of the belief that social betterment will be achieved through individual good will rather than through organized church efforts or political action. A privatized religious piety and concern for institutional growth through a spiritual ministry to church members' personal needs has obscured the church's mission to act corporately—to collectively attack systemic injustice. Many seem to believe naively that if we get right with Jesus, the world's problems will disappear.

An either/or mentality continues to distort our lives and confuse our understanding of the church. Piety and politics, religious experience and prophetic action, personal contemplation and social witness are continually pitted against each other, although the Christian faith calls for the integration of inner growth and outer change.

Piety in one sense is a neutral word. Ed Farley in *Requiem for a Lost Piety* defines Christian piety as a pattern of being and doing that rises out of a specific interpretation of the Gospel. For some, the Christian life is a privatized, otherworldly, anti-intellectual, emotional affair, which traditionally has been called *pietism* and is, from my perspective, a misinterpretation of the Gospel. Authentic Christian piety is individual *and* corporate, otherworldly *and* this-worldly, intellectual *and* emotional. It is expressed throughout every aspect of our daily lives, giving our actions their explanations, our attitudes their justification, and our beliefs their foundations. Christian piety is the church as the body of Christ reflectively acting in the world on behalf of the good news that God's kingdom is indeed among us. Piety without politics is, therefore, barren, while politics without piety is soulless. That is why St. Teresa of Ávila provides us with a model for the Christian life.

In the year 1515, Teresa, a child of the Spanish aristocracy, was born in a palace in Avila. Educated by Augustinian nuns, at 15 she entered a Carmelite monastery. Shortly thereafter a mysterious paralyzing illness obliged her to return to her family. On her recovery she once again returned to the convent. There she led a typically lax moral life, enjoyed a well-appointed suite, entertained friends, and regularly left the cloister to visit aristocratic ladies.

Her behavior was not uncommon, for an endemic sickness of the soul and moral laxity existed throughout the church. It was a difficult time to be nurtured into Christian faith and life. Most succumbed to the world's ways. However in 1555, at the age of forty, while praying before a statue of Christ, Teresa experienced a conversion, a transformation, a falling in love, and a subsequent opening of her eyes and ears to that which lies beyond the boundaries of our usual ways of knowing. From that moment on her prayers brought her into God's very presence. Divine communication, visions, and ecstasy followed. The life of perfection beckoned and as a faithful response she determined to find a house where disciplined contemplation and the simple rule of life would be strictly observed.

In the face of strong opposition from both church and state, she singlehandedly began to carry out her plan. In 1562 she founded the convent of St. Joseph in Ávila and wrote her first book, *The Way of Perfection*.

The subsequent years were filled with both contemplation and labor. Facing one difficulty after another, she built, reformed, and restored numerous convents and priories. At the same time her religious life deepened. In her later years she accepted the responsibility of prioress at Ávila, where she wrote *Foundations for Life* and, at sixty-seven, peacefully died.

St. Teresa was a woman of strong character, shrewdness, and great practical ability. As a writer, her influence was epoch-making. Her combination of mystic religious experience with ceaseless prophetic activity as writer, politician, reformer, and organizer makes her a classic instance for the contention that the highest contemplation is not incompatible with great practical achievement. In fact, in her life the two went together, each supporting and embracing and necessitating the other.

We humans are spiritual beings intended to live an integrated life of religious experience and prophetic action. Spiritual life is a life of faith that unites our beliefs, attitudes, and behavior. John Macquarrie in *Paths in Spirituality* defines spirituality as the practice of faith. Authentic Christian spirituality is a quality of both interior and exterior life in relationship to Christ and the Gospel. Spirituality as such is neither exclusively practices such as prayer or good works, nor is it an inner life blind to social and political realities. Rather, Christian spirituality is the common life of the Christian community informed by authentic piety.

Dimensions of our spirituality have been suppressed but not destroyed. Eventually they will emerge and seek to express themselves, for the spiritual quest demands wholeness.

To maintain an equal emphasis on religious experience and prophetic action in parish life will not be easy. The forces of our day work against us. Our blessings are curses. In the United States the church is a voluntary association. Thereby it is free to witness against the social order and engage in action to transform society. But in order to maintain its economic viability it must seek and attract members. To do so, an appeal to the masses through noncontroversial, self-serving activities seems necessary.

Second, we live within a religious pluralism. This pluralism is a natural outcome of religious freedom and can expand and enhance our various limited understandings. But it also creates a situation in which people are unable to accept universals, norms, or authority. All truth becomes relative and recedes into the private consciousness. A loss of the social dimensions of truth and the privatization of life ensue.

Third, urbanization with all its complexities has begun to dominate American life. Historically, cities have been the seed beds of new thought and change, but they have also evolved a world of specialization. Responsibility is divided. Typically, we depend on the specialist to have the answers and we tend to distrust our own convictions. Further, religion and the church become only one aspect of life, one specialized area of experience set apart for a particular function divorced from others. This situation is further complicated by the rapidity of change which leaves us without a meaningful past or future; by the bombardment of ceaseless problems, which leaves us numb; by the breakdown of effectiveness in problem solving, which leaves us feeling helpless; and by the dehumanization of life, which leaves us individually wounded and in need of a caring community. No wonder the church is asked and expected to bring comfort, not affliction, escape, not involvement!

Fourth, expanded and improved technology has made many past impossibles possible. But it has also fostered a society centered on *things*, possession of which becomes the goal, so that we become what we consume—things rather than persons. We concentrate on having rather than being. In this setting, faith logically becomes a possession, whether it is understood as personal living, a body of knowledge, or the experience of the spirit. Faith as an expression of what we are and do as members of a community is dulled, if not denied. Combined with our historic separation of the spiritual and material, our individualistic understanding of human nature, and our otherworldly understanding of salvation, it is difficult for our churches not to encourage religious experience and discourage prophetic action as the ends of Christian individual and corporate life.

Perhaps that is why the 1973 "Chicago Declaration" of evangelical Protestant Christians is so significant:

> As evangelical Christians committed to the Lord Jesus Christ and the full authority of the Word of God, we affirm that God lays total claim upon the lives of his people. We cannot, therefore, separate our lives in Christ from the situation in which God has placed us in the United States and the world.
>
> We confess that we have not acknowledged the complete claims of God on our lives.
>
> We acknowledge that God requires love. But we have not demonstrated the love of God to those who suffer social abuses.
>
> We acknowledge that God requires justice. But we have not proclaimed or demonstrated his justice to an unjust American society. Although the Lord calls us to defend the social and economic rights of the poor and the oppressed, we have mostly remained silent. We deplore the historic involvement of the church in America with racism and the conspicuous responsibility of the evangelical community for perpetuating the personal attitudes and institutional structures that have divided the body of Christ along color lines. Further we have

failed to condemn the exploitation of racism at home and abroad by our economic system.

We affirm that God abounds in mercy and that he forgives all who repent and turn from their sins. So we call our fellow evangelical Christians to demonstrate repentance in a Christian discipleship that confronts the social and political injustice of our nation.

We must attack the materialism of our culture and the maldistribution of the nation's wealth and services. We recognize that as a nation we play a crucial role in the balance and injustice of international trade and development. Before God and a billion hungry neighbors, we must rethink our values regarding our present standard of living and promote more just acquisition and distribution of the world's resources.

We acknowledge our Christian responsibilities of citizenship. Therefore we must challenge the misplaced trust of the nation in economic and military might—a proud trust that promotes a national pathology of war and violence which victimizes our neighbors at home and abroad. We must resist the temptation to make the nation and its institutions objects of near religious loyalty.

We acknowledge that we have encouraged men to prideful domination and women to irresponsible passivity. So we call both men and women to mutual submission and active discipleship.

We proclaim no new gospel, but the gospel of our Lord Jesus Christ, who, through the power of the Holy Spirit, frees people from sin so that they might praise God through works of righteousness.

By this declaration we endorse no political ideology or party, but call our nation's leaders and people to that righteousness which exalts a nation.

We make this declaration in the biblical hope that Christ is coming to consummate the Kingdom and we accept his claim on our total discipleship till he comes.

It is as a witnessing community that the Christian church is best understood. The church is to be the vehicle of God's mighty deeds transforming all of human life, an historical agency through which God is remaking the human world. Prophetic action is at the heart of the Christian life.

The church of Jesus Christ has only one mission in this world—the

social, political, economic world of our experience—as it extends
from the personal place where we live to the uttermost parts of the
earth. Within this world, where the majority of people live in severe
disunity, deprivation, poverty, hunger, and injustice, the church
bears the social imperative of being faithful to the mission of its Lord.
Christ's mission brought good news to the poor and called all people
to repentance, proclaimed release to the captives, recovery of sight to
the blind, liberation to the oppressed, and announced the arrival of
God's rule. His words *and* deeds witnessed to God's coming community. With Jesus, a new start, possibility, hope, and power had
arrived. Those bold enough to confess the name of Christ are commissioned to live in and for God's Good News; to live under the
judgment and mercy of the Gospel to the end that God's will is done
and God's community comes; to live as whole persons in conscious
loyalty to the conviction that Jesus is Lord; to seek always and
everywhere justice and equity, peace and unity, liberation and the
well-being of all persons and all creation.

The church is the bearer of this Gospel tradition. As such it is called
to be responsible to God and accountable to the historical context in
which it finds itself. Obedient, steadfast, faithful Christian life
necessitates prophetic action in the *polis*. Why is it that we need
continually to reaffirm this truth and cajole people to even consider
it, let alone to live accordingly? Perhaps because those of us who have
taken the social claims of the Gospel seriously have tended to neglect
religious experience and those who have remained to affirm religious experience have correspondingly done likewise with prophetic action and politics. My contention is that they belong together.
One without the other makes the Christian life a lie.

The Christian community is to live consciously in the presence of
the God who acts in history through persons and communities; it is
historical corporate life lived in a conscious awareness of God's redeeming and empowering presence, just as it is also life lived in the
political, social arena on behalf of justice and peace. It is the world of
piety and politics; it is the unification of deeply personal religious
experience and social prophetic action that remains at the heart of
Christian life.

Chapter 3

Conversions

Take a few minutes to reflect back over your life and your pilgrimage of faith. Think about the moments and the processes by which you grew gradually and also were significantly changed. Then record three major influences and events in your faith biography. Note especially the influential persons and public events that led to significant change in your understanding and expression of Christian faith.

*   *   *

The Christian life results in part from nurture in a Christian community of faith (see my book, *Will Our Children Have Faith?*). Faith as I am using the word is not simply knowledge of God or a relationship to God, it is rather an action in response to God, a centered reflective action of the total personality that assumes various styles in terms of our growth and development. Persons who live in a nurturing environment assume the characteristics of an ever expanding and more complex expression of faith. Faith grows as one passes, in turn, through each style of faith and continually meets the needs of that style. Of course, nothing about this process is natural. If the particular needs of one style of faith are not met, growth is stunted. Figure 3.1 is a diagram describing the characteristics of four styles of faith.

My contention is that until the needs of affiliative faith are met a person cannot acquire those characteristics necessary for prophetic judgment and prophetic action. I further contend that the church has inadequately satisfied these foundational needs. When Harvey Cox studied the appeal of and the functions played by the variety of cult and sect groups attracting youth today, he saw in our young people a deep desire for community, for profound religious experience, for

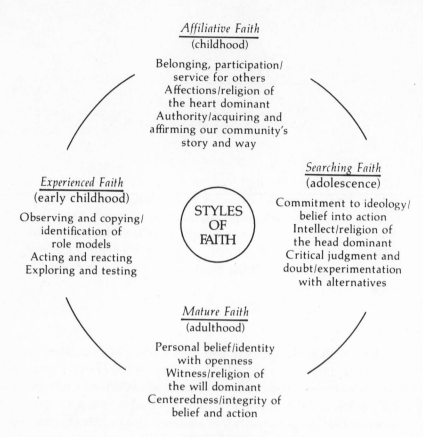

Affiliative Faith
(childhood)

Belonging, participation/
service for others
Affections/religion of
the heart dominant
Authority/acquiring and
affirming our community's
story and way

Experienced Faith
(early childhood)

Observing and copying/
identification of
role models
Acting and reacting
Exploring and testing

STYLES
OF
FAITH

Searching Faith
(adolescence)

Commitment to ideology/
belief into action
Intellect/religion of
the head dominant
Critical judgment and
doubt/experimentation
with alternatives

Mature Faith
(adulthood)

Personal belief/identity
with openness
Witness/religion of
the will dominant
Centeredness/integrity of
belief and action

Figure 3.1

something worth giving one's life to and living one's life for. These are the distinctive characteristics of what I have called affiliative faith. Since these needs are never fully satisfied or left behind, it is important that church life nurture them as well as those characteristics of searching and mature faith.

If you will recall my short biographical sketch of St. Teresa of Ávila, you can grasp her pilgrimage in faith. As an exemplary Christian life hers might also be helpful to describe distinctive Christian characteristics. St. Teresa trusted God. She firmly believed that God raised Jesus from the dead. She was convinced that nothing could destroy her life or separate her from Christ her Lord. She was secure and confident in spite of the insecurity of her society and personal life.

She had courage because she had experienced God and was convinced that she was not alone, that God was with her and would support her no matter what occurred.

St. Teresa was significantly aware of, and troubled by, her sin and unworthiness; yet she had profoundly experienced the in-spite-of love of God. She had experienced during private prayer and at the Eucharist the grace of God so that all of her life was transformed as she lived in that grace. She knew that she was loved, however unworthy, accepted, though unacceptable, and was therefore able to accept, affirm, and love both herself and others.

St. Teresa had a clear sense of her identity as a follower of Jesus Christ and a member of his church. She had been named and adopted into Christ's family. She identified herself with the community of Christian faith and within that community she had experienced the call of Christ to vocation.

St. Teresa was so secure in her own identity and in Christ's promises that she was a perfect example of the open mind. She was open to new experiences and to the opinions of all others, including her enemies.

St. Teresa had hope. She believed that God had given her a commission and that God would see her through. No barrier was too great, no opposition too strong, no illness too debilitating to discourage her. She firmly believed that God's will would be done. There was reason for hope and peace even in the midst of trial and tribulation.

St. Teresa was ready and willing to make personal sacrifice for the public good. She understood and was committed to taking up her cross and following after Christ her Lord because she had experienced her own crucifixions and resurrections.

St. Teresa exemplified the integrity of belief and action. The dissonance she had experienced during her earlier years was, after her conversion, replaced by correspondence.

St. Teresa focused her life on the future. She lived by and for her visions.

Now all these characteristics are the gift of a life of authentic piety and religious experience. None can be neglected in the nurturing of Christian life. Nevertheless, nurture alone was not sufficient in her life. Similarly, if the church today is to unite religious experience and prophetic action, thereby fulfilling its mission in the world, it will also be concerned with the transformation of persons and congregations. Many of our churches have become mirrors of secular culture. A new reformation is mandated. A new emphasis on conversion or transformation needs to accompany the old emphasis on nurture and formation.

Only through transformed lives will we be able to fulfill our mission of being Christian with others in the world. There is nothing natural about living the Gospel; indeed by the world's standards it is madness. Recently I read a newspaper account of an old man who after his retirement devoted himself to cleaning the floors of his church. He was known for his loving concern for people and his dedication to the life of prayer. His wife, however, regarded his piety and devotion as strange. One day while at Mass he had a vision and Jesus spoke to him saying: "Go and sell all you have and give it to the poor." He emptied his pockets into the poor box and set off on a pilgrimage. When he failed to return home his wife notified the police who located him some 40 miles from home and at his wife's insistence had him admitted to a mental hospital. He made no protest, but simply told his story. The psychiatrist thought him harmless and his wife reluctantly brought him home.

Some sixteen-hundred years earlier another man in a church in Alexandria heard the very same words during the Eucharist. He immediately set off for the desert and a life of heroic discipline until his death. His name was Anthony. Many followed him, and he established the first Christian monasteries, which were, we need to remember, major economic, social, and political forces in their day. As we know, St. Anthony was canonized; the other man was nearly certified. It may not be easy to tell the difference between destructive patterns of psychosis and the creative madness of St. Anthony or St. Teresa, but we ought not to neglect the importance of visions and conversions for the life of religious experience and prophetic action.

All too rarely have we used the word *conversion*, and all too frequently *evangelism* has been understood as a membership campaign. However, until we find a place for evangelism and conversion within the church, our corporate life will remain impotent and piety and politics estranged. Indeed, without converts the church will have difficulty being a community of either piety or politics.

Evangelism, as I am using the word, refers to the process by which the Christian community of faith, through the proclamation of the Gospel in word and deed, leads persons inside and outside the church to a radical reorientation of life — conversion. Evangelism is not indoctrination. It is testifying through transformed lives to the acts of God both within and without the community of faith. When we evangelize we witness through word-in-deed to the acts of God in Jesus Christ. Without this witness to the Lordship of Christ, to the good news of God's new possibility and to the Gospel's prophetic protest against all false religiosity, the church loses its soul and becomes an institution of cultural continuity maintaining the status quo rather than being an institution of cultural change living in and for God's coming community. Evangelism is best understood, therefore, as the means by which the church's life is transformed and her people become a body of believers who receive the Good News and are willing to give themselves to the cause of historically mediating God's reconciling love in the world.

It is hardly possible for anything less than a converted, disciplined body of believers in Jesus Christ to be the historical agent of God's work in the world. Christians are not born. Neither are they simply made, formed, or nurtured. Conversion — a reorientation of life, a change of heart, mind, and behavior — is a necessary aspect of mature Christian faith whether one grows up in the church or not. The church can no longer maintain the illusion that child nurture in and of itself can or will kindle the fire of Christian faith either in particular persons or in the church as a whole. We can nurture persons into institutional religion, but not mature Christian faith. We do not gradually educate persons to be mature Christians. To be a Christian is to be baptized into the community of the faithful, but to be a mature Christian is to be converted from ordinary ways of life to the way of the community of the New Age.

Conversion implies the reordering of our perceptions, a radical change without which no further growth or learning is possible. Conversion therefore is not an end, but a new beginning. It is a reorientation of one's life, a deliberate turning from indifference, indecision, doubt, or an earlier form of piety to enthusiasm, conviction, illumination, and "new" understandings and ways. Conversion is not to be understood only in the sense of a shift from no faith

or another faith to Christian faith; it is also an essential dimension in
the life of all baptized, faithful Christians.

Those who have been baptized as children and reared in the
church also need to experience conversions. Christians must fully
internalize the faith of the church and affirm their own faith by being
confronted with the choice of whether or not they accept or reject the
authority of the Gospel. Since Christian maturity and conversions
never exist apart from human maturity or development, we ought
not to impose the demands of adult faith and conversions on those
who lack the prerequisites of human maturity, nor should we think
of conversions as events or as happenings at one particular moment;
it is more typically a process. Conversion then is best understood as
an adult phenomenon, a significant aspect of the long gradual process of growth and maturation of faith by Christians within the
Christian family, a repeatable experience.

Authentic Christian life is personal and social life lived on behalf of
God's reign in the political, social, economic world. One cannot be
nurtured into such life — not in this world. Every culture strives to
socialize persons into its particular world view. The culture calls
upon its religious institutions to bless the status quo and calls upon
its educational institutions to see that persons accept it.

But God calls people to be signs of Shalom, the vanguard of God's
community. The conviction that such countercultural life is our
Christian vocation in but not of the world underscores the need for
our transformation.

Death and resurrection, repentance and becoming, describe the
experience of the Christian. As St. Paul wrote to the Corinthians,
"When anyone is united to Christ, there is a new world; the old order
has gone and a new order has already begun" (2 Corinthians 5:17
NEB). This talk of transformations, or conversions, may leave us a bit
uneasy, but let us never forget that education itself is best understood
as a transforming experience whereby our thoughts are reshaped and
our actions informed by new perceptions. The purpose of Christian
education is to evoke the possibility of turning from and toward by
confronting us with the decision not to continue with the way things
are and the decision to be as our Creator and Redeemer intended.

However, it is well to remember that this occasion or process of
illumination demands that we also wrestle intellectually with the

faith of the church. For too long we have ignored the intellectual demands of mature faith. The religion of the heart may come first, but the religion of the head needs to follow. Moral decisions and actions require the development of the intellect. While doubt may ensue, it is out of this struggle of the soul that illumination emerges. Needless to say, the hard intellectual study of our tradition and its implications is essential to mature Christian life and action.

Chapter 4

Pray Without Ceasing

Imagine that you are the art director of a magazine. You are about to design the cover of the next issue, and you want that cover to communicate both the theme of the issue and its meaning. The theme is prayer. There is only one thing you cannot do; you cannot use the word *prayer* on the cover. Proceed:

Table 4.1

Next, write what you believe is a model prayer for Christians to pray. Do not use the Lord's Prayer.

And last, describe a situation or occasion in which you believe you were praying most fully.

*   *   *

It is more than likely that the twentieth century will never be known as the age of prayer. It may in fact be remembered as the era of retarded consciousness. We have lost or forgotten the experience of God that lies at the heart of Christian faith. Still, we long and search for some sense of the divine: witness the renewed interest in the occult, Eastern religion, meditation, and personal religious experience. Something in us well knows that we are more than rational beings, that truth is more than reason can prove. Even we moderns are *homo religiosus.* Prayer and ritual are still basic expressions of our humanness.

Aquinas wrote: "Prayer is the peculiar proof of religion." Faith, in Luther's judgment, was "prayer, nothing but prayer." Baron von Hugel concluded that "prayer is the essential element of all life." Schleiermacher observed: "To be religious and to pray are really the same thing." Friedrich Heiler declared that "prayer is the heart and center of all religion." In fact, what most distinguishes a religious institution from other voluntary, ideological, or service institutions is its claim to prayer.

Still the word *prayer* lacks clarity. Some think of prayer as distressed cries to the heavens, others a formality before meals and meetings or an experience on mountain tops. Prayer for some is a spontaneous emotional discharge and for others a fixed rational formula to be recited. Prayer, as I am using the word, is a generic term to describe every aspect of our conscious relationship with God. Prayer is the method of the spiritual life — daily existence lived in relationship with God, the daily activity of living in the presence of God through adoration, confession, praise, thanksgiving, and petition/intercession.

The spiritual life then is an historical life lived with a conscious awareness of God's presence; it is life so lived that our minds, hearts,

and wills and God's are united in common historical reflective action. Surely this understanding rules out prayer in which the world
or the self is depreciated or denied, in which the human personality
is dissolved or absorbed into a unity with an otherworldly reality.
Prayer is not a negative process moving us out of our normal state or
condition, a passive resigned contemplation of otherness, nor a striving after emotional ecstasy through the extinction of thought or voli-
tion. Prayer is ultimately an ethical activity. History is the peculiar
province of God's revelation and fellowship. Blessedness of life with
God is life in this world; in our daily lives we meet and have communion with God.

For such an understanding of prayer to prevail we need to recover
the proper place of religious experience and thought. The popularity
of the charismatic and Jesus movements are evidence of our neglect
of that experience, but that does not mean that we ought,to turn
uncritically to speaking in tongues, pseudomysticism, exotic forms
of meditation, or uncontrolled emotion. The switch from doctrine
and dogma to silence or *glossalalia* is no solution. Nor is the switch
from formal institutional and ceremonial life to simplistic emotional
commitment to Jesus. Spiritual euphoria without social action may
be religious, but it is not Christian. Personal ecstasy is no substitute
for social justice. "Thy kingdom come" is an essential petition of
Jesus' prayer. *Maranatha*, "Come Lord Jesus," is the central petition
of the early church. Both call us to live in a conscious relationship to
God's kingdom. Prayer or true religious experience, for the Christian, is living in communion with God in the midst of personal and
social history-making.

The Christian life focuses upon the spirit of God in us and in the
world; its quest is for an active unity with the God of history. The
climax of the Christian life is not enlightenment but unification with
the will and activity of God. Christian prayer assumes both an historical awareness and the integration of the receptive and active modes
of consciousness.

Numerous examples of prayer in the Bible support this understanding. The Scriptures assume an historicist perspective. Operat-
ing from that perspective, the prophets used their intuitive ability to
hear the voice of God and their intellects to proclaim a judgment on
the people for their lack of righteousness and on the nations for their

lack of justice. Moses' experience with the burning bush led him to bring to his people a vision and a message of liberation. Jesus' struggle at Gethsemane led him to make a conscious decision to choose the foolishness of the cross. The awareness of the presence of Christ in the breaking of bread at Emmaus led the disciples to lives of apostleship and martyrdom. Paul's experience on the road to Damascus and in the presence of Ananias led him to change from a persecutor to defender of the faith that in Christ there is neither Jew nor Greek, male nor female, slave nor free—a truly revolutionary position yet to be fully realized.

Each of these experiences represents a unity of a new worldly consciousness of God and of praxis, which is reflective worldly action, according to God's will. Each is a true example of the life of prayer.

If prayer is no longer satisfying or if God seems no longer real, it may be because we have turned prayer into speaking formally to God. Only prayerfulness, a radical love of God and neighbor, is fully satisfying. Listening to God and serving God is true prayer. Prayer implies an engagement with the world, a wrestling with the principalities and powers. Prayer is never an escape from the world or its trials and tribulations. Prayer is a way of life, a relationship with the God who acts in history, lived day by day.

Prayer is not so much telling God as it is listening and responding to God, to God's will, to God's actions. It is not found in attempts to manipulate God or change God's will; it is rather listening and answering God's call to newness of life and action with God in the world. In the Scriptures, prayer is primarily a thanking and recalling of God's presence in one's life and in history, not primarily asking God for something. God is asking something of us. God is seeking to have us live in and for God's coming community. Prayer is our getting our lives right with God. It ought not to be an exceptional experience.

Every prayer prayed either through daily acts or symbolic acts (ritual prayers) is political. That is why our symbolic acts as well as our lives need to be continually under judgment. Both express a political viewpoint; either they inspire social imagination and vision or they reconfirm our taken-for-granted world. They advocate some particular understanding of human life as well as make assumptions about the nature and goals of human history. They either numb or sensitize us to God's will and way, either support and bless the world as it is, or judge and inspire us to live for a new world, God's coming community.

"By their rites you will know them" is not mere rhetoric. We cannot do without worship. We humans are made for ritual, and in turn our rituals make us. Faith and ritual cannot be separated. That is why, when the prophets sensed that the people had forsaken their faith, they attacked their rituals. But when the people had lost faith they called them to return to their rituals.

There are no people or communities without their symbolic actions. Some are formal, that is, written down, and others are informal, or unwritten. Both are repetitive and orderly. In this sense there is no difference between the formal rituals of Roman Catholics and the informal rituals of Baptists; either can act to bless and sustain the way things are in the world, inducing persons into accepting society as it is, or either can act to inform our imaginations and transform our ordinary ways of seeing and understanding, causing us to live for change.

Our life of communal ritual prayer can be best judged by how well it transforms our daily lives, granting us visions, hope, and power to live as persons and groups informed by the Gospel. Our ritual prayer life can be best judged by whether or not it moves us to engage in systemic social change, to act on behalf of justice, to struggle with the social forces, institutions, and systems that dehumanize persons and groups.

Christian prayer enables us to engage in Christian spiritual life. It unites piety (our experience of a relationship with God) with politics (our prophetic active relationships with our neighbors and the world). It is expressed both in ritual acts and in daily life.

Chapter 5

The Work of the Community

List a few of the concrete prophetic actions taken by or supported by your denomination during the past year on social, political, or economic issues, and state your congregation's response. For example, the United Church of Christ acted to support the Wilmington 10 in North Carolina. One congregation responded by writing a letter to the governor of the state requesting that he pardon them.

Action   Response

Next, list the concrete political, social, or economic actions taken by you and/or your congregation during the past year on an issue such as racism, sexism, peace, economic justice, poverty, or hunger. Do not list study groups or service projects such as "meals on wheels" or fund raising for hunger.

My Actions   My Congregation's Actions

Last, outline your congregation's Sunday liturgy (order of worship), and next to each item listed as part of the service explain what understandings of Christian life you think it typically supports. For example: prayers—individual concerns of parishioners and/or social concerns for justice in the world.

Liturgy   Understandings

When you have finished, compare and contrast your congregation's understandings of Christian faith, as supported in its worship, with your congregation's actions in the community.

*   *   *

Liturgy, properly understood as the work of God's people, unites ritual (symbolic actions) and daily life (personal and social action). Our symbolic actions, if they are Christian, will inspire and motivate persons and the community to act in the world on behalf of God's will for justice, equity, unity, peace, and the well-being of all. Similarly, our personal and social actions in the world, if they are Christian, will be informed by, as well as demonstrate, a conscious loyalty to Christ and the Gospel.

Without rituals to support them, there is no meaningful personal life or sustained political, social action. Liturgy, the activity of the community, necessarily integrates symbolic action and social action. Each needs and supports the other. To deny either one is to deny the whole. Liturgy, the life and work of the community, includes discipleship within the faith community, telescoped in rituals, and apostleship in the world, expressed through personal and corporate service and action. Insofar as we neglect ritual we starve and discourage social action. By emphasizing social action to the neglect of ritual we lose our roots and inspiration. Insofar as we neglect social action we distort the faith and create unholy rituals. By emphasizing escapist, individualistic, otherworldly rituals we make Christian life in the world all but impossible.

There has been and perhaps always will be a certain tension in the church between the attitude that emphasizes meditation, contemplation, mystic experience, and ritual prayer in a space withdrawn from the world and its temptations and the attitude that emphasizes good works in the world. The responsibility of the community of Christian faith is to keep these attitudes from becoming estranged.

The church is best understood as a community of the adopted and called. For too long we have thought of the church as a company of those who have received a special reward—salvation. God is gracious to all who seek salvation—Jews, Hindus, Muslims, Humanists—because God is the sort of God whom Christ revealed. Christians are simply those whom God has named and commissioned through baptism to witness to the salvation he has brought to all the world. What we have received is not a special blessing, but a special burden and responsibility, namely, to live for the salvation of all humanity.

Christianity is essentially a response. When we were baptized we were baptized into a twofold vocation—the worship of God and the redemption of humanity. Nevertheless, we will be able to live in and for this Gospel only insofar as it becomes living truth for us. This is why no matter who we are or what we do, we need to reflect, contemplate, withdraw, meditate, and participate in corporate prayer. We will know if we have met Christ in these moments of worship by our fruits. If we have met Christ we will have a new way of looking at life, and the outward manifestation of our transformation will be seen in our working to change at least a portion of the world in which we live.

As Christians, singularly and corporately, we are meant to become involved in the transformation of the world. Christian involvement is the fulfillment of the liturgical act. To be an apostle is to be an actor. Recall that the New Testament book is entitled "The Acts of the Apostles," not the talk, beliefs, or experiences of the apostles. To be Christian the church must be willing to accept identification with the world in which it finds itself.

Most people who do not accept the church are not refusing the church but misrepresentations of it. Many well-informed, sensitive, concerned, alert, intelligent people who do not accept Christ are rejecting what should be rejected. They are rejecting a perversion of Christianity, a false interpretation of it given to them by people who claim the name of Christ but who do not understand the Gospel's radical demands for political, social, and economic life.

Of course, few church folk would deny that Christians are to be committed to the human development of all people, the realization of human rights, the elimination of economic, social, and racial injustice, the peace of the world, and the physical well-being of all people. But the rub comes in our seeming inability to act upon those commitments, especially where we live. How much easier it is to write pronouncements about the denial of human rights in the Soviet Union or raise money for hunger in India than to address, through systemic change, the needs of our neighbors within our own cities and towns. How much more difficult it is to critically judge and reform our world-denying personal, inner-peace rituals; to acquire an understanding of institutions, social structures, systems, and processes of life; and to strive to make corporate moral decisions and action informed by Christian faith!

To live the liturgy, to do the work of the people of God, is to gather for word and sacrament, to celebrate the Lord's Supper, to live the Eucharist, to make intelligent informed decisions, and to act upon them in ways that can affect life in a complex, interdependent, sinful, sick world. As the Body of Christ we are called to so live our life in community that we might bring a vision, anticipation, and hope to the world; that we might bring wholeness and well-being to all persons; that we might bring acceptance and compassion to all who live in brokenness; that we might bring challenge and judgment to all who distort God's desire for life; that we might be an embodiment of justice, righteousness, reconciliation, and peace in a cynical world and a concrete witness to a dream in a practical world. As Luther put it, wherever you see God's Word preached, believed, confessed, *and acted upon*, there is the true church. The church cannot exist without word and sacrament, but neither can the church be faithful to Jesus Christ if it does not embody that word and sacrament in the world.

Throughout its history the church has striven to be faithful to the Gospel by adjusting its understanding of mission in each time and place. To reconcile the demands of being faithful to God in Christ amidst a hostile world the early Christians shaped their own lives so that their community might be a foretaste of God's promised kingdom. As the book of Acts witnesses, the church was a company of those of one heart and soul. No one possessed anything, for all was held in common. There was not a needy person among them, for everyone sold their possessions and the community distributed them according to people's needs. Further, they acted toward their neighbors with self-giving love and witnessed to a new spirit. In a world that forced them into isolation, they relegated their efforts to the change of their own small communities rather than to wider social reform.

However, following Christianity's emergence as the official religion of the West, the church gained a new sense of social obligation that encompassed all of society. The church now chose to initiate reform within the institutions of society and, further, promoted the idea of a unified Christian civilization whose spirit would penetrate and renew the fabric of society as a whole. The dream was valid, but soon the world's understandings and ways began to infect the church. Instead of transforming the world, the church tended to mirror it. The call soon came for reform. Still affirming an integration of Christianity and society, they sought better means to infuse the society with the Christian vision.

But the Christian civilization upon which these attempts rested began to erode. Secularization and the growth of an urban, technological society created a new era in which the church was perceived as essentially irrelevant. Increasingly the church was isolated from political, economic, cultural life. It appeared as if the church was to become a minority faith in a secular world.

If the church is to fulfill its calling to transform the world it must become a systemic force in the struggle for justice and peace. The church must take the world with utmost seriousness, must identify with that world and its needs without being assimilated into it, and must strive to engage in actions of love using power on behalf of God's coming community in the context of the social order. As a community called apart to sustain its understandings of the Gospel through symbolic ritual acts, the church must also engage corporately in every action that might renew the earth and bring peace, justice, and liberation to all humanity. To become a community of love, power, and justice—a community of vision, hope, and action in-but-not-of the world—is the vocation and work of a community of Christian faith. That is what is means to live the liturgy.

Chapter 6

Making Moral Decisions

Complete the following questionnaire by checking the appropriate boxes:

Figure 6.1

The Christian faith

Item	Supports	Opposes	Says Nothing	I Don't Know
abortion				
capitalism				
justice				
safety				
individualism				
physical health				
uniting all people				
war				
socialism				
peace				
pollution				
nutrition				
euthanasia				
free enterprise				
economic security				
equality				
freedom				
capital punishment				
ownership of private property				
community				
poverty				
prejudice				

Review your responses and defend each by appealing to Scripture and Christian tradition.

How did you rate abortion, euthanasia, war, capital punishment? Each is related to the issue of life and death. Were you consistent? What principle or norm did you use in making your choice or decisions?

If a particular social policy required that you choose between the values of freedom and equality, which would you choose? Why?

* * *

Social action is the art of working together for the purpose of transforming society. It implies efforts to reshape social institutions and public policies. It is judged by its effectiveness in achieving political, social, and economic justice for all. However, one of the crises of our day is that the church has tended to reduce or blur whatever is distinctively "Christian." In the measure to which this is so, we have more or less accommodated ourselves to American values characterized by a broadly defined secularism that excludes serious attention to the distinctiveness or uniqueness of Christian faith. A church that would engage in Christian social action must first of all become aware of what it means to be Christian.

The question of morals is the question of right and wrong. The question of values is the question of what are desirable ends and means for life. Ethics answers the question of why these particular choices are right or desirable. That is, ethics provides us with norms for our decision making. Beyond ethics is the question of authority. Ethics may provide us with norms, but the contexts or situations in which we make moral and value decisions are complex and always crying to be heard in their particularities. Our ultimate authority provides us with a means for mediating between these sometimes conflicting claims.

For the Christian the ultimate authority is the Word or action of God in Jesus Christ: the principle of love, power, and justice. Affirmed in the conviction that Jesus is Lord, the Christian is called to act intentionally in conscious loyalty to God's love as revealed in the passion and resurrection of Jesus Christ. As believers in Jesus Christ and members of his church we have no detailed or concrete information on what we ought to do in any or every particular situation. But we know we are to live accountable and obedient to the authority of the Gospel, and thereby under a social imperative to act under certain norms or principles by which we discover for what ends and by what means we are to live. Basic to this Gospel tradition are convictions concerning the sanctity of the natural world, human life, and community, each of which convictions provides us with norms (not rules or laws) for holiness.

To affirm God as Creator is to affirm that creation is good. We are to live in harmony with the natural world and we are to care for it creatively. Therefore, the norm of Christian moral decision making is to preserve and value all human life and the natural world. Other actions may be made necessary by particular situations so as to be faithful to the liberty and authority of the Gospel, but the burden of proof is always on those who in any way would disrupt the natural world, stymie the creative process, or take human life.

To affirm God as Redeemer or Liberator is to affirm the value of human life. Despite our sinfulness God values us. What God loves we should in no way despise. Persons are never to become means or objects. Humanity is of greater value than any ideology. No end justifies any means. The social worth of a person is not to be based on her/his endowments. Indeed the equality of all human life is to be affirmed. Our value cannot be determined by any qualities of life we have or lack. Instead we must begin with the interests of those least endowed. Again, other actions may be made necessary by particular situations so as to be faithful to the liberty and authority of the Gospel, but the burden of proof is on those who in any way would disvalue human life.

To affirm God as Sustainer or Advocate is to affirm that we are meant for community. Unity and fellowship among all persons is the goal of life. Love, seeking the good of the near and distant neighbor through personal sacrifice and social justice is the norm. God's intention is for the oneness of the human family. Sexism, racism, classism, nationalism are a denial of that community. Particular actions may be made necessary by particular situations so as to be faithful to the liberty and authority of the Gospel, but the burden of proof is on those who in any way would disrupt community or cause a separation among peoples.

A Christian conscience is an activity of the whole person, within a community of faith and in conscious loyalty to the conviction that Jesus is Lord, passing moral and value judgments on what is faithful. A Christian conscience does not provide detailed information on how to address the world's social problems. The Gospel is not a political or economic theory. But the Christian message says something fundamental about that for which life is to be lived. Once again, the Christian message does not give any detailed information as to how our social problems should be tackled technically or justice achieved. But the Gospel does say something about how life is to be lived.

The church can and must become a community of moral discourse, a community not living for its own benefit, but for the good of all human beings. The church cannot avoid being actively involved, through both proclamation and action, to provide moral leadership in a confused, disheartened world. The Christian faith makes endurance possible even when there appears to be no progress; it makes courage possible in the struggle for justice, freedom, and peace; it makes hope possible when there appears to be nothing to be hopeful about.

The important question is: What is a faithful act? For example, in 1869, I.Q. tests were developed. It was the first time anyone had conceived of a way to take individual differences seriously. Today they have become the involuntary means by which minority people are kept out of the mainstream of American society. Are I.Q. tests good or not? I do not know, but I suspect that while it might have been faithful to favor them in 1869, it is now faithful to oppose them. Each generation must seek afresh for a faithful response to its time.

A renewed concentration on the liberty and authority of the Gospel should provide us with common ground on which to deal creatively with conflict and overcome unnecessary polarizations. Only then will we avoid the dangers of overvaluing social action and undervaluing the necessity of personal renewal or overvaluing personal devotion and religious experience and undervaluing social commitment and prophetic action. Only then will we all remember that whoever preaches or lives only half the Gospel is no less a heretic than the person who preaches or practices the other half. Together we must defend the Christian faith and maintain the continuity of the tradition; we must be true to the task of study, critical judgment, and the need to examine our beliefs and lives afresh. Only then shall we abide by the truth of Jesus Christ and be prepared to reform and renew the church for social commitment and action wherever the Gospel of Jesus Christ demands.

Part Two

FORMS
OF
FAITHFULNESS

Chapter 7

Memory and Vision

Relax a moment, close your eyes, and try to envision a perfect world; it need not be practical or even feasible, only consistent with the Scriptures and what you believe is God's dream for the world and all its people. Then record the highlights of your vision. If you can link the vision with a book, story, or chapter from Scripture, indicate the source.

Now, reflect on the past. Strive to recall those significant historical events that you would attribute to the will of God, that is, those actions you believe contributed to God's dream for the world.

*   *   *

To speak of the Word of God is to speak of the actions of God. God's Word is in God's deeds. The God of the Christian faith is the God who acts purposefully in history; the God who calls the world into covenant with him that his will might be done; the God who has given us the vocation to act with him so that his community, which has come and is coming, will yet come in all its fullness.

Thus it is that the church is a community of memory and vision. To know the Word of God is to intimately, personally, and experientially understand the world and our lives in terms of God's intentions and mighty deeds. To fulfill our covenantal vocation is to live faithfully in the present, in grateful awareness of the past, and hopeful anticipation of the future.

The significance of the scriptures is their record of both our primal memories and visions. It is the story of our foreparents' attempts to understand God's will and to live accordingly. While some of the Biblical precepts are culture-bound, the Biblical story, culminating in the life, death, and resurrection of Jesus Christ, provides us with a world view or perspective for understanding all history and our lives within that history.

While it is important for us to learn this story, it is even more important for us to make this story our own. That is what it means to know the Word of God. And the test of whether or not we know God's Word is whether or not we sense God acting in our lives and history today. If we have truly internalized the Christian perspective on life, we will live lives informed and inspired by this experience.

Within a Christian frame of reference, the Bible's whole thrust is to the future. The past is powered by the future, a future understood in terms of the past. The community of faith is called to live between memories and visions. The Bible is, therefore, primarily a book about the future, God's future rooted in God's past actions and promises. The challenge facing us in our day is this: to become a tradition-bearing community living faithfully toward God's vision.

To know God's Word is to live for the day when all creation is one, when every creature is in community with every other, living in harmony, security, and plenty, seeking the joy, good, and well-being of every other creature. It is a future in which the human family is united around the will of God and under the Lordship and fellowship of Jesus Christ. All creation and all creatures share a common destiny and blessing to live without division, hostility, fear, drivenness, and misery. It is a vision that encompasses all of reality, a this-worldly, historical, socio-politico-economic reality. The future is with justice and righteousness. Salvation, wholeness, and health is its blessing. To know God's Word is to live in and for God's rule within a caring, sharing, joyous community. All afflictions and suffering, all oppression and lostness, all inequality and estrangements have passed away. Liberation, freedom and unity, harmony, order and abundance, peace and health are to be shared in community. It is a new heaven and a new earth in which all humanity dwells together with God; and darkness, death, mourning, and pain are no more.

And what is it that sparks such an imagination? It is our awareness of God's mighty deeds. Faith in the actions of God is central to the Biblical understanding of God and God's relation to the world. These acts of God are best understood as related to the course of history. God liberates and saves, makes whole and healthy, brings justice and mercy. These are the mighty acts of God. In retrospect, we can discern where in particular these acts have been made manifest, but any and every particular act cannot be attributed to God. To affirm the actions of God in history is to live in the faith that history is going somewhere, that life is ultimately intentional and purposeful. This is not to have faith in a God who gives full attention to our every complaint, miraculously saves us from all difficulties, or responds to all our requests by invading nature and history. Rather it is a faith in the Lord of heaven and earth, whose purposes we cannot fully fathom and whose ways we do not always understand, but who does provide us with a vision of the future that is to be and in mysterious ways directs the course of that history toward fulfillment. The mystery of that faith is remembered and lived in a story: God made a promise to our foreparents, liberated our people who were in bondage in Egypt, fed us bread in the wilderness, brought us to a good land, made us into a people, came to us in Jesus Christ, conquering sin and death and reconciling the world to himself; and gave us his Spirit that all might have life and have it abundantly.

When that memory and vision become part of our lives we will know the Word of God.

Chapter 8

Understanding the Word

Read the following passage of Scripture:

Comfort, comfort my people,
    says your God.
Speak tenderly to Jerusalem
    and cry to her
that her warfare is ended,
    that her iniquity is pardoned,
that she has received from the Lord's
    hand double for all her sins.
A voice cries:
"In the wilderness
    prepare the way of the Lord,
    make straight in the desert
    a highway for our God.
Every valley shall be lifted up,
    and every mountain and hill be
    made low;
the uneven ground shall become level,
    and the rough places a plain.
And the glory of the Lord shall be
    revealed,
    and all flesh shall see it together,
    for the mouth of the Lord has spoken."
A voice says, "Cry!"
    And I said, "What shall I cry?"
All flesh is grass,
    and all its beauty is like the flower
    of the field.

> The grass withers, the flower fades,
>> when the breath of the Lord
>> blows upon it;
>> surely the people is grass.
> The grass withers, the flower fades;
>> but the word of our God
>> will stand for ever. *(Isaiah 40:1-8)*

Answer the following questions:
1. When or in what season of the year would you read this passage in church?
2. What New Testament lesson would you read with it?
3. What hymn would you sing with it?
4. Using this passage as your text, suggest a sermon title and the three points you would make.

Now, read the following:

Imagine that you are living in the sixth century before Christ. The kingdom of Israel has fallen to non-Jewish hands, and the Jews are scattered throughout the Empire. You are a Gentile. For you, life is good. You have wealth, freedom; you worship the local gods. The Jews, from your perspective enjoy economic and religious freedom. You are uneasy, however, because you wonder whether the Jews constitute a threat to your way of life in that their religion seems so bound up with political aims. It is your new year's festival, a time when you celebrate your religion and the good life you have been given by the political-economic system under which you profitably live. Isaiah, a Jew, comes before his people and preaches the Isaiah 40:1-8 sermon. What do these words mean to you in such a context? Do you like what Isaiah says? Why? Why not? Are there two different messages here? Now consider your own life today—are you more like the Jews or the Gentiles in Isaiah's day?

Go back and read your responses to questions 1 through 4 at the beginning of this exercise. Record your reflections on the responses that follow.

Considering who I am and the people in my congregation, I would use this Isaiah passage during Advent. I would use the following New Testament lesson with it:

My soul magnifies the Lord,
and my spirit rejoices
    in God my Savior,
for he has regarded the low estate
    of his handmaiden.
For behold, henceforth all
    generations will call me blessed;
for he who is mighty has done
    great things for me,
and holy is his name.
And his mercy is on those
    who fear him
from generation to generation.
He has shown strength with his arm,
he has scattered the proud in the
    imagination of their hearts,
he has put down the mighty
    from their thrones,
and exalted those of low degree;
he has filled the hungry
    with good things,
and the rich he has sent empty away.
He has helped his servant Israel,
    in remembrance of his mercy,
as he spoke to our fathers,
to Abraham and to his posterity
    for ever. (*Luke 1:46-55*)

I would sing the hymn "The Voice of God Is Calling."

The voice of God is calling
    Its summons unto men;
As once he spake in Zion,
    So now he speaks again:
Whom shall I send to succor
    My people in their need?
Whom shall I send to loosen
    The bonds of shame and greed?

We heed, O Lord, thy summons,
  And answer: Here are we!
Send us upon thine errand;
  Let us thy servants be.
Our strength is dust and ashes,
  Our years a passing hour,
But thou canst use our weakness
  To magnify thy power.

My sermon title would be: "Repent: Change Your Life." My three points:
1. God's Word brings justice, which is judgment and mercy.
2. God judges us for our racism, sexism, classism.
3. God offers mercy to those who change their lives.

Do you agree or disagree with my understandings? Why or why not?

* * *

For those of us who acknowledge God's Word, it is incumbent that we ask: What does this Word mean? To interpret, to make sense of God's actions and the witness to the divine-human encounter preserved in the Scriptures is to ask: How are we to live with the Bible? The Bible is addressed to the church. Its purpose is to make ready for the Lord a people prepared (Luke 1:17). As such, when properly interpreted, it is a present resource for faith.

The Bible is the church's book. It was created, shaped, and passed on over a long period of time. Amidst changing needs, problems, and questions it sometimes provided a word of judgment, sometimes words of mercy for the community of faith at crucial junctures in its history. It appears as if a different word was appropriate at different times. The prophet Micah proclaimed: "and they shall beat their swords into plowshares and their spears into pruning hooks" (4:3). But Joel called upon his hearers to "beat your plowshares into swords, and your pruning hooks into spears" (4:10). In John's Gospel, Jesus says, "Peace I leave with you; my peace I give to you; not as the world gives do I give to you" (14:27). But in Luke's Gospel, Jesus says, "Do you think that I have come to give peace on earth? No, I tell you, but rather division" (12:51). It appears as if you can quote the Bible to support every possible position.

The Scriptures are filled with paradoxes. In the New Testament we are told that salvation is available in the name of Christ alone, but we are also told that it is not those who say "Lord Lord," but those who do the will of God who will enter the kingdom. In one sentence we are told that the only way to God is through the name of Christ. In another we are told that the only access to God is through the loving service of the neighbor in need. How then do we interpret the Biblical message in our day? Perhaps the clue is found in Ecclesiastes, where the preacher proclaims: "For everything there is a season, and a time for every matter under heaven . . . a time to kill, and a time to heal; a time to break down, and a time to build up . . . a time to love and a time to hate . . . " (3:1 ff.).

If this is the case, then the key to interpreting the Word of God is to be found in knowing how to hear it. At different times in history God spoke a particular word to a particular people living in a particular situation. No matter what our present condition there is a word for us within God's Word, if we will face our true human condition and seek out the word God addresses to us. For too long we have gone to the Bible in search of the message we want to hear rather than the one we need to hear. It is not wise to search the Bible for proof-texts to support our present limited understandings and prejudices. Anyone can do this and indeed find justification for individual prejudices or behavior. It is better to search for those passages that counter and confront us with new understandings. That seems to be the way God has always acted and spoken. When God's people were without hope, they received a word of hope. When they were oppressed, God liberated them, but when they were oppressing, God brought them a word of judgment. When they were prosperous and proud, God humbled them.

Bible study is not so much a process of questioning the Scriptures as it is a process of permitting the Scriptures to question us. Faithful interpretation of God's Word calls us to repentance and invites us to a changed perception of life. We need to take the Bible more seriously or we will miss its claim upon our lives and fail to recognize its authority and peculiar transforming power. To interpret God's Word rightly is to experience a changed consciousness.

The Bible calls the church to understand its rightful identity and proper mission. For too long we have used the Bible as a drug and pacifier. The central invitation of the Bible is to new life. It is concerned with faithful relationships between God and people, between God's community and all the world. It invites us into a dialogue, sometimes painful and sometimes consoling.

Earlier we pointed to justice as a major theme in the memory and vision of the Christian faith community. This word of justice must be understood as a word of both judgment and mercy. Without this paradoxical Word, grace is cheap and the Gospel an opiate of the people. Isaiah 40 is a perfect example, as is Mary's song, of this twofold message.

To the repressed, suppressed, and oppressed there is no message with more comfort than these two passages. But we cannot afford to ignore the fact that this message of comfort also announces the downfall of the powerful and comfortable. Mary's song and Isaiah's pronouncement both announce a revolution. The first will be last and the last first.

God is putting things right. He is bringing mercy to those who need mercy and judgment to those who need judgment. The difficult and demanding task of the faithful is to discern which word is addressed to them. In either case, however, there is joy and hope in believing. For those denied God's intentions by the actions of human beings and national governments, there is the hope and joy in knowing that they have not been forsaken. God has taken their side and will see that his intentions for all people will be granted them. For those who have already received God's blessings and have enjoyed them at the expense of the rest of God's creation, there is also a word of hope and joy, for God's judgment is salvation. We are invited to repent and to act in response to our neighbors' needs. Mercy is the opportunity to join God in bringing hope and joy to the oppressed, suppressed, and repressed. Through transformed lives we too then know hope and joy.

Too often we hear the Word of God wrongly. We must learn to listen to the right message. Jesus did say to Satan, "Man does not live by bread alone." But when faced with the hungry, he commanded his disciples to feed them. For too long we have listened to the wrong words and missed God's Word. To be faithful is to discern the signs of the times, to acknowledge our true condition in the world, and to seek out that transforming Word of God which is justice for all people. To do so is to interpret the Word of God from the perspective of the Gospel.

Chapter 9

Living the Word

Below are listed various aspects of the church's ministry. Define each and summarize what and how well your congregation is doing in terms of that definition.

Evangelism

Stewardship

Social Action

Worship

Pastoral Care

Fellowship

Administration

Education

* * *

What does it mean to live as the family of God? What is the church's ministry? To answer these questions is to understand what it means to live the Word of God. The Christian community of faith is called to live in the memory and vision of God's Word; to corporately sense which of the words in God's Word are addressed to the community so that it might respond faithfully; and to be a sign to the world of God's coming community. The mission of the church is the compelling risk to live our common longings for the Gospel of Jesus

Christ so that the community of God may be realized. Our ministry includes all those ways of believing, being, and behaving that contribute to this mission.

While we may fall short of our calling, and indeed are always in need of reform and renewal, we cannot afford to be unclear as to our ministry. In the light of God's Word our vocation is clear:

Evangelism is the church witnessing through word and deed to its faith in the transforming power of God's good news.

Stewardship is the church expressing through its life and proclamations God's will for individual and corporate life in the world.

Social service and action is the church engaged in the loving use of power through political and economic actions on behalf of God's coming community.

Worship is the church being empowered for mission and ministry through the opportunity for confrontation with and commitment to the Gospel.

Pastoral care is the church ministering to both the material and spiritual needs of all people.

Fellowship (church life) is the church providing a sign and foretaste of God's coming community.

Administration is the church planning, organizing, and directing its life so that it can best be faithful to God's Word.

Education is the church becoming aware of God's will for life, judging the church's faithfulness and equipping/stimulating itself to engage in mission and ministry.

For too long we have privatized our faith and hence distorted it. For too long we have busied ourselves with an institutionalization of the Gospel. Evangelism has been focused on individual converts and institutional growth. Stewardship has been fund raising. Worship has been for personal solace. Pastoral care has been counseling for church members. Fellowship has been to provide a club-like environment for those who desire to escape the world's trials and tribulations. Education has been for the nurturing of children into church membership. Administration has been for maintaining a peaceful, prosperous organization. And social action has been either avoided or turned into patronizing good deeds.

To live the Word is to be faithful to the Gospel, but we have turned it into institutional survival. We have busied ourselves with our own internal needs and lost our soul. We have copied every new fad and mirrored the culture. To live God's Word is to acknowledge our corporate sin and to repent. God's Word calls us to conversions, that is, over and over again to turn and live in a new covenant with God. Living God's Word has to do with transformation and new starts, with the loyalties we embrace, the tasks we accept, the values we serve, the ways we live our lives together, and the ways we act in the world.

The purpose of the church is to authentically celebrate the Eucharist in community and live the Eucharist in the world. Education for ministry is to prepare, stimulate, and strengthen the community to undertake the ministry implied by our faith and baptism. The ministry of the church belongs to all baptized Christians and includes any kind of service by which Christians, individually and corporately, exercise their particular skills and gifts, however humble, to help their fellow Christians and all fellow humans in the name of Christ.

To experience the Word of God is to let God work within the church that the world might know the power of the Gospel and believe.

Chapter 10

Embodying the Word

Below is a passage from the Gospel of Mark. Read it carefully and then write, in your own words, a paraphrase of this verse using as few of the original words as possible:

> The time is fulfilled, and the kingdom of God is at hand; repent, and believe in the gospel. *(Mark 1:15)*

Following this proclamation, Jesus calls forth disciples. Write a newspaper advertisement for disciples:

* * *

A new day has dawned, and God's dream for creation is now possible. Change your life and begin to live for that good news. That was and is Christ's message. Of course it is a ludicrous word, but Christ's true disciples are those who are foolish enough to believe it and wise enough to live in and for it.

To embody the Word is to know it, interpret it rightly, to live it. Those who know, interpret, and live the Word of God will be known by their *doing* of it. To embody the Word of God is to join in the activity of God. The church is the agent of God sent to carry out God's purposes for the redemption of the world. The church does not exist in or for itself. The church exists to carry out Christ's mission in the world.

History is becoming; it is a divine-human event. The Christian church is an institution within that history. It has no alternative other than to become historically involved, to take responsibility for the character and quality of human life. It is impossible for the church either to be a spectator or to be neutral. The church will either support life as it is or change it. Not to act is to support life as it is, to be without dreams, without hopes, without faith in the Gospel. A choice cannot be avoided. We either take our place in the process of change or we maintain our present conditions. Unless we honestly believe that God's will is indeed done and God's community has come to all its fullness we have no choice.

Still, getting the church to do God's Word is most difficult. We give lip service to peace, justice, equity, community, health, love, brotherhood and sisterhood, unity and the well-being of all persons. But we do little concretely to realize our words. Kind words and even good works are not sufficient. Personal goodness, long the understanding of religious life, is insufficient to answer the complex problems facing an industrialized, urban society. Surely the time for well-meaning intentions, desires, and pronouncements has passed. The times require a prophetic church engaged in transforming social actions on behalf of the Gospel.

It cannot be put anymore succinctly than in the words of James: "Be doers of the word, and not hearers only, deceiving yourselves" (1:22). What good is it if we say we have faith but do not express it in deeds? Faith without those deeds is dead, indeed it does not exist. For too long we have accepted the notion that to be a good Christian is to be active in a congregation and to be personally righteous in daily life. The church is not the place where we are to live out our faith. It is the place where we are empowered to act on behalf of sustained efforts to accomplish social change. The prime work of faith is to be done in the world. Social service is necessary, but not sufficient for Christian life. Social change is incumbent upon us.

The world today confronts Christians with enormously complex and difficult problems: poverty, racism, economic injustice, hunger, war, pollution, and others beyond measure. Short-term efforts are insufficient to deal with them, as are all personal efforts. We need to unite together to address the basic transformation of worldwide social, economic, and political systems. Unless the church has opted to forsake God's Word it needs to unite in efforts to affect systemic social change.

The issue is not whether the church can know the right thing to do, nor whether the church can really make any significant difference, nor whether the church ought to be involved in political, social, and economic life. The issue is simply whether the church will be faithful in embodying God's Word. The God of the Christian faith has always been the God who acts in history. God acted in Jesus Christ to transform all human life by bringing into history God's rule and community. The church that would be the Body of Christ has no option other than to be that transforming power in contemporary history. The mission of the church is to corporately act in the world so that the world might have a sign of the Gospel. To live in the hope of the Gospel is to search for where God is acting in the world and to join God in those actions. Those who have hope founded in Christian faith will engage in social actions that challenge the evils of society—poverty, ignorance, disease, oppression, injustice, war, and prejudice—and create through political action human alternatives consistent with God's will.

To embody God's Word is to stop contributing to identified social ills; to take a stand on social issues; to raise a prophetic voice against injustice; to take positive action; to influence public opinion; to join with others in working for justice; to become a political, economic force for systemic change; and to use power lovingly on behalf of the transformation of the world.

We live in a society of institutions. We are shaped by these institutions and we can shape them. We live within a world of systems. They frame and express our understandings and ways of life. We can change them. The church is one institution living within a political, social, economic system. We have an obligation to make our society just and humane by influencing that system. If God's vision for the world is to be realized, the church needs corporately to do God's Word. The call ought to be clear. What remains is our response.

Chapter 11

The World of Catechesis

List all the places in your church where persons learn what it means to be Christian.

List all the places in your church where persons are prepared and stimulated to be Christian in the world.

Now write an evaluation of how well your church is doing in these matters.

Describe an occasion in which you had an experience of significant learning.

Attempt to outline the steps or stages in this learning experience.

* * *

Historically, in describing her educational ministry, the church has differentiated between catechetics and catechesis. Catechetics deals with the ends and catechesis the means. In the United States catechesis has been fundamentally understood as schooling and instruction. The church school is an important enterprise, but it is a limited and insufficient understanding of catechesis.

The word catechesis—*katechein* in Greek, literally to echo, reproduce, imitate, or pass on something given—has a long and noble history. The word describes what is essentially a pastoral activity, which includes every aspect of the church's life. Catechesis is a process intended to both recall and reconstruct the church's tradition so that it might become conscious and active in the lives of maturing persons and communities; a process by which persons learn to know, internalize, and apply the Word of God in daily individual and corporate life. As such, catechesis aims to enable the faithful to meet the twofold responsibility that Christian faith requires: community with God and neighbor.

Catechesis, therefore, is a life's work shared by all those who participate in the ministry and mission of the Christian faith community. It values the interaction of a community of believers who are striving to be faithful in-but-not-of the world. Catechesis asks the fundamental question: How can we be Christian together in community and in the world? To answer this question is to understand the means by which we become Christian within a community of faith. As such, catechesis occurs wherever divine revelation is made known, faith is enhanced and enlivened, and persons are prepared for their vocation in the world. Catechesis intends to help us to understand the implications of Christian faith for life, to critically evaluate every aspect of our individual and corporate living, and to become equipped and inspired for faithful activity in church and society.

Catechesis challenges us to be responsible for disciplined, intentional, faithful, obedient life together. Catechesis includes all deliberate, systematic, and sustained efforts within a community of faith that enable both the individual and the community to live faithfully under the judgment and inspiration of the Gospel, to the end that God's will be done and God's kingdom come. Catechesis focuses upon knowing God or critically understanding and interpreting the Word of God; loving God, or owning, internalizing, and living the Word of God; and obeying God, or applying, acting, and doing the Word of God.

This does not mean that every aspect or activity in church life is catechesis; it means that catechesis is an aspect of every activity within the church. For example, social action is not catechesis, but catechesis is an important aspect of social action. Catechesis helps the church to understand faith's requirement for political action in the world; to critically evaluate the church's political activity or inactivity from the perspective of Christian faith; and to prepare the church (as a community) to act faithfully in the world.

Catechesis implies that the whole life of a congregation offers times and places in which Christian learning may occur. It is holistic;

that is, it is a broad-visioned approach aimed at discovering and developing the many ways that learning and growth occur in the community.

For too long we have depended upon church schools and church-school classrooms for our educational efforts. New means and modes need to be explored and developed. Intentional groups with shared and integrated learning aims need to be initiated. We cannot permit intentional learning to become separated from life. It is not reasonable or wise to separate knowing, interpreting, living, and doing the Word into discrete categories and separate systems. To do so and then to permit congregations to choose one or another of these approaches is a denial of the wholeness of the Gospel. Embodying the Word can never be understood as one option among others. To do the Word is the end of all catechesis. While catechetics or church schooling may be able to differentiate between various identifiable educational goals and design educational experiences accordingly, catechesis understands Christian growth and development as a gestalt, that is, from an integrated, holistic, rather than a particularistic point of view. Educational approaches can support and enhance one another, but only if catechesis is seen as prior and primary.

In planning for catechesis, one might consider approaching people where they are in existing boards, committees, church groups, and other natural gatherings in the church and community. However, it may be difficult to attract persons to existing groups; it may be better to begin new ones and to bring together persons with similar needs, concerns, hurts, and questions. Quality of experience is more important than quantity. Weekend retreats or three to five intensive sessions may be better than one hour a week for a year. Of course, full commitment to participation is essential. Begin where people are: with their needs, doubts, interests, abilities, understandings, and existential situations. Include them in planning. Act with (not to or for) others. Make sure that your aims include new behaviors; that is, there should be something significant or new to think, feel, or do as a result of having been together. Make sure that persons practice the behaviors implied in your aims.

Catechesis can occur in any pastoral activity where persons are striving to be Christian together; it simply calls for experiences and environments where groups of believers can interact with the tradition and one another. Any number of contexts apply: committee and board meetings; coffee hours; building programs; special ceremonies; preparation for baptism, first communion, confirmation; preparation for marriage, moving, retirement, death; choir rehearsals or music programs; retreats; family life; bazaars; lunches and suppers; art shows; dramas and dances; groups where people work; social events; car pools; neighborhood and home events; trips to museums, shows, events; counseling sessions; preparation for worship; after school, on vacation, or during holidays; conferences and camps; outdoor events; travel tours; volunteer service projects; social action groups; mass media events; special interest groups; residence groups; publications; community conflict situations; church meetings; crises in the lives of people; new-member events; special occasions in people's lives.

Today there is a new demand for a knowledge and understanding of the tradition—"a return to the basics." But just as important is the need to interiorize the tradition. And most important is the ability to apply our tradition to the urgent issues facing our society today.

An integrative approach to education (catechesis) that unites religious experience and prophetic action; unites knowing, interpreting, living, and doing the Word; and unites piety and politics is essential for an effective Christian mission.

At the heart of an integrated catechesis is a vital, tradition-bearing community of the Word. In the past, when a dynamic faith community did exist, the Sunday school made an important contribution to the church's educational ministry. As a vital faith community lapsed, the church school found itself unable to adequately fill the gap. Where a faith community enhanced and enlivened by catechesis exists, the church school can make an important contribution. But without a vital catechesis, church schooling has little soul. The challenge before us is to evolve new forms of catechesis.

Chapter 12

Learners and Learning

To know is to have an intellectual or attitudinal awareness. To learn is to integrate our awareness into our behavior in ways that influence and shape our decisions and actions. Training alters our behaviors without increasing our intellectual insight or our authentic awareness. Only learning produces a true change in our total way of living.

The Greeks differentiated between three ways of knowing. *Theoria* was contemplative or reflective knowing acquired from an objective distance; its legitimate end was understood as knowledge. *Poiesis* was skill development; through unreflective participatory activity new ways of acting were acquired. Activity was its reasonable end. *Praxis* combined participation and contemplation, action and reflection, and so made possible living the truly ethical life. Only the latter, I contend, is satisfactory for learning in the Christian church.

Learning is a profound event that leads to significant change in our total life. It involves four related steps or stages:

1. An awareness of a starting point, a conscious acknowledgment of one's present state and its foundation in past experience. Such an awareness necessitates a psychological readiness and openness to new experience. Typically this occurs best when we are placed in a situation where a critical awareness of our condition can surface and old understandings and ways be challenged.

2. A significant experience best taking place away from one's home environment, though shared in community with others. If we are truly to learn, something must happen to jar us from our starting point, from home base, from our present stability. This something is a significant experience, an externally or internally produced conflict in our understandings and ways. The dynamic of this confrontation or conflict forces us to reevaluate our present patterns of life. The experience need not always be dramatic, but

will usually entail a feeling of dissonance. This event or combination of events makes us aware of the inadequacy of the way we have been living and the ideas that have determined our behavior. It also provides us with alternative options for the future. If the experience is significant enough, we feel the need for change.

3. Reflection: A serious confrontation with our lives as lived demands reflection in order to acquire a new sense of stability and wholeness. Such reflection can precipitate decisions that indeed do change our whole lives in identifiable ways. It therefore results in learning. Reflection is thinking about, contemplating, weighing, wrestling with new understandings and ways. Prayer is an obvious integral aspect of reflection. Like significant experiences, reflection can take place in a matter of moments, but more than likely will take place over a period of time. In any case, it is best done in community with others who are also striving to resolve their dissonances.

4. Assimilation: Learning is not complete until we eliminate our old ways and integrate our new understandings. The end of assimilation is a public commitment to our new life-style and its particular behaviors. Action, the undertaking of specific activities consistent with our new commitment, is an expected outcome. Significantly, in time, these new actions become part of who we are, and we are open to further learning, so that we start the process over again.

Learning requires that we know where we are and how we are living; it makes available significant experiences that confront us with alternatives; it provides us with space and time to reflect on the implications of these alternatives and to make decisions; and it makes possible assimilation and action on our new commitments.

Catechesis is the process of learning within a tradition-bearing community of Christian faith, so that the Word of God might be known, interpreted, lived, and done through new sensitivities to God's revelation, through the enlivenment of faith, and through the integration of life as vocation into new behaviors in the world consistent with the Gospel's demands. To be Christian with others in the world through the integration of piety and politics requires such learning. And such learning is at the heart of church reform and renewal!

Part Three

PATHWAYS
TO
FAITHFULNESS

Chapter 13
Preparing to Learn

Thus far we have established a theological foundation and educational method for a curriculum of church reform and renewal, that is, for living the integrated spiritual life of authentic Christian piety, uniting religious experience and prophetic action. In this section we will offer *one* possible model for catechesis consistent with these understandings. However, this model will be viable only insofar as those persons involved share the convictions voiced in the earlier parts of this book. Therefore, the learning design that follows assumes an exposure to and reflection upon Parts One and Two. Those who desire to proceed should gather to review and modify the rest of this book for their particular use.

It would be a mistake to conceive what follows as a "bag of tricks" ready for use and sure success. The model is best understood as a limited resource for learning. Some sections, for the purposes of example, are more complete than others. Some lack the specificity necessary for immediate use. Each step, however, is consistent with the understandings presented earlier. For example, the first retreat is intended to produce a significant experience; the next two sections provide an opportunity for reflection; the retreat and final planning sessions are an opportunity for assimilation. Still, each section as presented is only intended to be suggestive. It would be an error to use the material unaltered. Indeed, it would be difficult, if not impossible to do so. My purpose is to provide an aid for educational planning, not a ready-made handbook.

The "Spiritual Life Retreat" described in chapter 14 focuses on the Christian tradition, personal faith, and the church's mission. Its aim is to evoke dissonance between our disintegrated lives of religious experience and prophetic action and to provide a vision of wholeness consistent with the Gospel. It is suggested as a Friday-evening-through-Sunday-morning event at a retreat or conference center. The next four two-hour sessions (chapter 15, "Church Life and Mission") were created to be conducted in homes where, in the context of prayer, the group who had attended the retreat might reflect on their actions as a community of faith in the light of the Gospel. Their aim is to help the community acquire a sense of mission. The four two-hour sessions in chapter 16 ("Analysis: Social Issues") encourage action and reflection. Their purpose is to help the group identify and reflect upon the social, political, and economic needs in their community that are confronting the Christian church. Chapter 17 describes another weekend retreat, whose aim is to provide spiritual exercises that will help persons to internalize their learnings and commit themselves to action. The last four two-hour sessions (chapter 18, "Community Action") suggest ways to acquire those skills necessary for faithful action in the world and a means to plan for action. (Note: A resource book, *A Social Action Primer* by Dieter Hessel, needs to be ordered in advance if this design is to be followed.)

My hope is that this model will facilitate your own development and planning of a learning design. Use it not as a gimmick, but as a resource to be adapted for your own use.

INTRODUCTION

This design represents an educational resource of 13 weekly two-hour sessions and two retreats for adults and/or youth. Normally, that involves a commitment of three months and two weekends, but you may discover you need more sessions to complete the design. Since each session is related to the ones that go before, commitment to full participation is essential.

Two or more persons, ideally the pastor and at least one lay person, are necessary for the leadership of this design. Participants should be enlisted from the congregation on the basis of concern for the development of their faith and a desire to live more faithfully in the world.

I would also recommend a series of preliminary sessions to introduce and discuss the first two sections of this book and thereby provide a necessary foundation for the educational design. The suggestions that follow are addressed to the person facilitating these introductory sessions.

SESSION ONE

In preparation for this first session distribute copies of *Inner Growth/Outer Change*. Ask all participants to read chapters 1 through 3 and to complete the exercises at the beginning of each chapter.

When you gather, do so in an informal setting, perhaps at someone's home. Make sure that participants are acquainted with one another.

1. Ask each participant to tell the group how he or she feels about the state of the church today. Have each person explain how he or she recognizes a Christian church. Have persons comment on their agreements and disagreements with the position presented in chapter 1.

2. Have each person share his or her triptych and Scripture verse from the opening exercise in chapter 2. Have the group list ways in which their personal understandings of the Christian life and the church are similar and different from the point of view expressed in this chapter.

3. Have the group discuss the question: Is it possible to live the Christian life without some transforming experiences? Then ask: How might we be helped to live the radical life of discipleship?

4. Have each person share a highlight of her or his faith biography.

It would be appropriate to close the session with the Lord's Prayer and refreshments.

Assign chapters 4 through 6 to be read for the next session.

SESSION TWO

Begin this session by reviewing the various opinions expressed at your first gathering.

1. Have participants share their magazine covers and experiences of prayer from the exercise at the beginning of chapter 4.

2. Discuss the understanding of liturgy as the work of the community presented in chapter 5. Further, consider how worship in your church supports or deters political, social, and economic action.

3. Have each person share an opinion expressed in the exercise at the beginning of chapter 6. How are moral decisions reached in your church? Consider the process of moral decision making expressed in chapter 6. How does it compare with the group's own convictions?

Close in an appropriate manner.

Assign all the chapters in Part Two, "Forms of Faithfulness."

SESSION THREE

Begin the session by reviewing the various opinions expressed at your last session.

1. Have each person share a vision as expressed in chapter 7. Discuss: Do you believe that God acts in history? What do you mean by these words? Ask selected persons to share their understanding of the Christian story.

2. Discuss: Do you agree or disagree with the interpretation presented in chapter 8? Why or why not? Ask each person: What word do you believe our church needs to hear today?

3. Have each person share his or her understanding of ministry as recorded in chapter 9. Discuss what needs to happen in your church to foster faithful ministry.

4. Have persons, in subgroups of two to four, compare paraphrases of Mark 1:15 and share their newspaper advertisements for disciples as presented in chapter 10. Discuss where your church succeeds and falls short on embodying or "doing the Word."

Close in an appropriate manner.

Suggest that those who fundamentally agree with the convictions of these first two parts read through Part Three and gather next week at an appointed time and place to plan a learning design.

SESSION FOUR

In preparation, read carefully the suggested retreat and other learning designs.

When you gather, begin by sharing your opinions expressed in the exercises of chapters 11 and 12 on catechesis and learning.

Then review the learning design which follows. Rework or revise where necessary and make assignments for leadership and other responsibilities. Plan dates, times, and places. Make sure that the group owns the design you adapt and is committed to participation.

Then discuss important unresolved issues or questions from the previous three sessions.

Close by having an evening meal or refreshments.

Chapter 14

A Spiritual Life Retreat

What follows is a contemplative/action retreat.

The form of this retreat may appear strange to those raised in the reformed, free-church Protestant tradition. It represents only one way to meet the aims of this weekend session. If you find the structure, the silence, fasting, and/or formal worship difficult for meaningful participation, then plan for more informal worship consistent with your own understandings and ways. Reorder the exercises or develop alternatives as you feel will best meet your needs.

Consider, however, that the very strangeness of this retreat format might provide the context for new significant experience. There is something meaningful about living for a short time in ways dramatically different from the usual. Silence and fasting can put us in a mood for new awarenesses. The seven liturgies, following the monastic hours, come from different traditions. The service of penitence is adapted from an Episcopal service that is also familiar to United Methodists. An alternative would be to use one of the penitential services in preparation for the Lord's Supper found in the Reformed tradition. Its purpose is to make us aware of the dissonance between what we believe and how we live. The next liturgy is taken from the traditional Moravian love feast and uses music familiar to the more evangelical churches. Its purpose is to unite us in a community of grace and to heighten our awareness of God's Holy Spirit. The third liturgy is the traditional Jewish Passover meal. It reminds us of our shared tradition. At 3:00 P.M. we celebrate a liturgy adopted from Taize, a Protestant monastic community in France, uniting Calvinist, Lutheran, and Roman Catholic elements. Its purpose is to remind us of true Christian witness. Vespers is adopted from a liturgy created by the African Churches for use at the World Council of Churches meeting in Nairobe. The baptismal renewal is adapted from an Episcopal service. Its purpose is to give persons the opportunity to reaffirm their commitment to the Christian life. For those who choose to awake at 1:00 A.M., Prayers for the World are adapted from a Roman Catholic liturgy. The Lord's Supper or Holy Eucharist is adapted from the liturgy of the United Church of Christ and is familiar to Presbyterians and other Calvinists. Other traditions will want to use their own Eucharistic prayers. The basic purpose is to refresh us for the Christian life. The exercises should be self-explanatory.

The retreat begins with a community supper. A substantial meal is suggested, because, after the evening party, the community fasts until after the Eucharist Sunday morning. It should also be explained that the retreat participants are to maintain the rule of silence except during worship and the community exercises.

Following supper the group should prepare for the retreat. Arrange an appropriate setting for all the liturgies, review the liturgies so that everyone is clear what to do when, and assign leadership where necessary. Also make sure that you have everything you need, such as basins, water, and towels for the footwashing. In fact, before setting off on the retreat, study this manual carefully and make sure that you have all the food and equipment necessary.

Once you are prepared and organized for the retreat and settled in your cabins for the night, have a party, play games, sing, eat, have fellowship together. Arrange for some signal to awaken people for the first service at 6:00 A.M. and then go to bed. The retreat follows; my directives assume that a minister or priest is the leader of the retreat. If this is not the case, you may need to change some of the words in the liturgies.

6:00 A.M.	A Service of Penitence
	Exercise: The Struggles of the Soul
9:00 A.M.	A Moravian Love Feast
	Exercise: Exploring the Faith
12:00 P.M.	A Freedom Seder
	Exercise: Body Time
3:00 P.M.	A Celebration of Christian Witness
	Exercise: Searching the Word
6:00 P.M.	A Service from the Third World
	Exercise: Living the Word

9:00 P.M.   A Baptismal Renewal
            Sleep
1:00 A.M.   Prayers for the World
            Sleep
6:00 A.M.   The Holy Eucharist or Lord's Supper

Following the Eucharist, prepare breakfast together. During breakfast reflect on your experiences.

A SERVICE OF PENITENCE

This liturgy begins standing around an altar table. Bold-face type is used for the community responses.

INTRODUCTION
The Lord is in his holy temple; let all the earth keep silence before him.

With what shall we come before the Lord, and bow ourselves before God on high? What does the Lord require of us but to do justice, and to love kindness, and to walk humbly with our God?

The sacrifice acceptable to God is a broken spirit; a broken and contrite heart, O God, you will not despise.

Let us pray.

Have mercy on us, O God, according to your steadfast love;
According to your abundant mercy blot out our transgressions.
Create in us a clean heart, O God;
And put a new and right Spirit within us.
Cast us not away from your presence;
And take not your holy Spirit from us.
Restore to us the joy of your salvation;
And uphold us with a willing Spirit.

Eternal God, in whom we live and move and have our being, whose face is hidden from us by our sins, and whose mercy we forget in the blindness of our hearts, cleanse us, we pray, from all our offenses, and deliver us from proud thoughts and vain desires, that with low-

liness and meekness we may draw near to you, confessing our faults,
trusting in your grace, and finding in you our refuge and our
strength; through Jesus Christ your Son. **Amen.**

God spoke all these words, saying,

"I am the Lord your God, who brought you out of the land of Egypt,
out of the house of bondage.

"You shall have no other gods before me.

"You shall not make yourself a graven image, or any likeness of
anything that is in heaven above, or that is in the earth beneath, or
that is in the water under the earth; you shall not bow down to them
or serve them; for I the Lord your God am a jealous God, visiting the
iniquity of the fathers upon the children to the third and the fourth
generation of those who hate me, but showing steadfast love to
thousands of those who love me and keep my commandments.

"You shall not take the name of the Lord your God in vain, for the
Lord will not hold him guiltless who takes his name in vain.

"Remember the sabbath day, to keep it holy. Six days you shall labor,
and do all your work, but the seventh day is a sabbath to the Lord
your God; in it you shall not do any work, you, or your son, or your
daughter, your manservant, or your maidservant, or your cattle, or
the sojourner who is within your gates; for in six days the Lord made
heaven and earth, the sea, and all that is in them, and rested the
seventh day; therefore the Lord blessed the sabbath day and hal-
lowed it.

"Honor your father and your mother, that your days may be long in
the land which the Lord your God gives you.

"You shall not kill.

"You shall not commit adultery.

"You shall not steal.

"You shall not bear false witness against your neighbor.

"You shall not covet your neighbor's house; you shall not covet your neighbor's wife, or his manservant, or his maidservant, or his ox, or his ass, or anything that is your neighbor's."

Hear also what our Lord Jesus Christ has said:

"You shall love the Lord your God with all your heart, and with all your soul, and with all your mind. This is the great and first commandment. And a second is like it, You shall love your neighbor as yourself. On these two commandments depend all the law and the prophets."

PRAYERS
(Kneel, sit, or stand as is your custom.)
Let us pray.

O Lord our God, from whom come all holy desires and just works, breathe into our hearts by your holy Spirit the gift of obedient faith, that we, knowing your will, may keep these words in our minds and hearts, and may do those things which are acceptable to you. **Amen.**

O God, the Creator of the universe,
Have mercy on us.
O God, the Liberator of the world,
Have mercy on us.
O God, Advocate of the faithful,
Have mercy on us.
For blindness to your truth and persistence in selfishness,
Have mercy on us and forgive us, O Lord.
For envy, hatred, and anger; for all evil thoughts and desires,
Have mercy on us and forgive us, O Lord.
For failure to love and serve our neighbor, for prejudice and contempt toward others,
Have mercy on us and forgive us, O Lord.
For neglect of worship and prayer; for indifference to your Word and your power,
Have mercy on us and forgive us, O Lord.

That you will strengthen your church in every land, and unite all people in true faith,
We pray you, O Lord.
That your church may strive not for her own safety, but for the world's salvation, seeking only your kingdom and your righteousness,
We pray you, O Lord.
That we your people may understand and believe your Word, and that our lives may bear testimony to your goodness,
We pray you, O Lord.
That we may rightly use your holy sacraments and be strengthened in body and soul by your heavenly grace,
We pray you, O Lord.
That all nations may live together in peace, and all persons dwell together in unity,
We pray you, O Lord.
That your comfort may uphold all who are ill, that your wisdom may give guidance to all who are perplexed or afraid, that your providence may sustain all who are in want or need, that each of your people may draw from you courage and faith to meet the struggles of life,
We pray you, O Lord.
O Creator, Redeemer, and Sustainer, ever one God,
Have mercy on us and grant us your peace. Amen.

Our Father in heaven:
　　holy be your name,
　　your kingdom come,
　　your will be done,
　　　　on earth as in heaven.
　　Give us today our daily bread.
　　Forgive us our sins,
　　　　as we forgive those who sin against us.
　　Save us in the time of trial,
　　　　and deliver us from evil.
For yours is the kingdom, the power, and the
　　glory, forever. Amen.

AFFIRMATION OF FAITH
(All stand.)
Let us affirm our faith:

I believe in God, the Father, the Almighty,
    Creator of heaven and earth.

I believe in Jesus Christ, his only Son, our Lord.
    He was conceived by the power of the Holy Spirit
        and born of the Virgin Mary.

He suffered under Pontius Pilate;
    He was crucified, died, and was buried.
He went to the dead.
On the third day he rose again,
    entered into heaven,
    and is seated at the right hand of the Father.
He will come again to judge the living and the dead.

I believe in the Holy Spirit,
    the holy Catholic Church,
    the communion of saints,
    the forgiveness of sins,
    the resurrection of the body,
    and the life eternal. Amen.

CONFESSION
Beloved in the Lord: If we say we have no sin, we deceive ourselves, and the truth is not in us. If we confess our sins, God is faithful and just, and will forgive our sins and cleanse us from all unrighteousness.

Humble yourselves therefore under the mighty hand of God, that in due time he may exalt you. Cast all your anxieties on him, for he cares about you.

Seek the Lord while he may be found, call upon him while he is near. Let the wicked forsake their way, and the unrighteous their thoughts; let us return to the Lord, that he may have mercy upon us, and to our God, for he will abundantly pardon.

God so loved the world that he gave his only Son, that whoever believes in him should not perish but have eternal life.

(Kneel, sit, or stand as is your custom.)
I now ask you, in the presence of God and upon the evidence of your own conscience:

Do you acknowledge your sinfulness and repent of your sins with contrite hearts?
I do.
Do you believe that God is willing, for Jesus' sake, to forgive all your sins?
I do.
Do you resolve to submit yourself in the future to the gracious direction of the Holy Spirit, so that you may no more sin willfully, but be enabled to follow after holiness?
I do.
Do you forgive those who have sinned against you?
I do.

Holy God, you formed us from the dust in your image and likeness, and redeemed us from sin and death by the cross of our brother Jesus Christ. Through the water of baptism you clothed us with the garment of righteousness and established us among your children in your community. But we have squandered the inheritance of your saints and have wandered far in a land that is waste. Especially we confess that we have sinned against you in thought, in word, and in deed. We have rejected your righteous will in choosing our own. You alone know how often we have sinned in wandering from your ways and in forgetting your love. Through our sinfulness we have separated ourselves from you and from our neighbor. Now in the presence of Christ we confess our personal sins . . .
(Silence.)
Therefore, O Lord, from these and all other sins we cannot now remember, we turn to you in sorrow and repentance. Receive us

again into the arms of your mercy and return us to the blessed company of your faithful people. Trusting in your great mercy, we ask your pardon. For the sake of your Son, Jesus Christ, forgive our sin. Send the purifying power of the Holy Spirit into our hearts, that from this day on we may live in the light of your love and may be at peace with you and with all people; through Jesus Christ our Lord. Amen.

You then, who after examining yourselves have penitence and faith, and who desire to forsake all sin and follow after Christian holiness, approach with me now the throne of grace. Receive again the assurance of God's redeeming grace: God so loved the world that he gave his only Son, that whoever believes in him should not perish but have eternal life. For God sent his Son into the world, not to condemn the world, but that the world might be saved through him. You may assuredly believe that if you turn to God in true repentance and faith your sins are forgiven, through Jesus Christ our Lord. **Amen.** *(Stand.)*

Glory to God in heaven,
    peace and grace to his people on earth.
We praise you for your great glory,
    we worship you, we give you thanks,
    Lord God, heavenly king,
    Almighty God.
Lord Jesus Christ, Lamb of God,
    only Son of God,
Who take away the sins of the world,
    have mercy on us;
Who sit at the right hand of God,
    hear our prayer.
You alone are the holy one,
    you alone are the Lord,
    you alone are the most high,
    Jesus Christ,
    with the Holy Spirit,
    in the glory of God. Amen.

Now may the God of peace, who brought again from the dead our Lord Jesus, the great Shepherd of the sheep, by the blood of the eternal covenant, equip you with everything good that you may do his will, working in you that which is pleasing in his sight, through Jesus Christ, to whom be glory forever and ever. **Amen.**

EXERCISE NUMBER ONE: *The Struggles of the Soul*
Be alone and in silence.
Reflect on your faith, your faith pilgrimage (how you became the person of faith or unfaith you now are), and your continuing struggles with the Christian faith.

Reflect on the following:
What does your faith have to say about acting in the world? What prophetic social actions have resulted from your faith?

At the onset of his ministry Jesus proclaimed the coming of the kingdom and called women and men to a complete change of heart and mind. What radical changes have taken place in your life as a result of your faith in Christ?

The Christian faith suggests that we may need to detach ourselves from dependence upon the dominant institutions and systems that surround us. It demands that we live a life that is quite different from the norm. Indeed, the Gospel intends to free us from domination by the world's understandings and ways. To what extent have you found this true in your life?

The Christian is to resist an otherworldly and privatized Gospel. To what extent has your faith in Christ empowered you to confront and combat those social forces that dehumanize life or support injustice?

Meditate and pray.

A MORAVIAN LOVE FEAST

HYMN: *Dear Mother-Father of Us All*
Dear Mother-Father of us all,
Forgive our foolish ways;

Reclothe us in our rightful mind;
In purer lives Thy service find,
In deeper reverence, praise.

In simple trust like theirs who heard,
Beside the Syrian sea,
The gracious calling of the Word,
Let us, like them, our faith restored,
Rise up and follow thee.

O Sabbath rest by Galilee!
O calm of hills above!
Where Jesus knelt to share with Thee,
The silence of eternity,
Interpreted by love.

Breathe through the hearts of our desire,
Thy coolness and Thy balm.
Let sense be dumb, let flesh retire;
Speak through the earthquake, wind, and fire,
O still small voice of calm!

With that deep hush subduing all,
Our words and works that drown,
The tender whisper of Thy call,
As noiseless let Thy blessing fall,
As fell Thy manna down.

Drop Thy still dews of quietness,
Till all our strivings cease;
Take from our souls the strain and stress,
And let our ordered lives confess,
The beauty of thy peace.

FOOTWASHING *(John 13:1-17)*
Now before the feast of the Passover, when Jesus knew that his hour
had come to depart out of this world to the Father, having loved his
own who were in the world, he loved them to the end. And during

supper, when the devil had already put it into the heart of Judas
Iscariot, Simon's son, to betray him, Jesus, knowing that the Father
had given all things into his hands, and that he had come from God
and was going to God, rose from supper, laid aside his garments, and
girded himself with a towel. Then he poured water into a basin, and
began to wash the disciples' feet, and to wipe them with the towel
with which he was girded. He came to Simon Peter; and Peter said to
him, "Lord, do you wash my feet?" Jesus answered him, "What I am
doing you do not know now, but afterward you will understand."
Peter said to him, "You shall never wash my feet." Jesus answered
him, "If I do not wash you, you have no part in me." Simon Peter said
to him, "Lord, not my feet only but also my hands and my head!"
Jesus said to him, "He who has bathed does not need to wash, except
for his feet, but he is clean all over; and you are clean, but not all of
you." For he knew who was to betray him; that was why he said,
"You are not all clean."

When he had washed their feet, and taken his garments, and re-
sumed his place, he said to them, "Do you know what I have done to
you? You call me Teacher and Lord; and you are right, for so I am. If I
then, your Lord and Teacher, have washed your feet, you also ought
to wash one another's feet. For I have given you an example, that you
also should do as I have done to you. Truly, truly, I say to you, a
servant is not greater than his master; nor is he who is sent greater
than he who sent him. If you know these things, blessed are you if
you do them."

*(With music in the background, conduct a footwashing ceremony. Have
each person wash the feet of the next person, beginning with the leader.)*

HYMN: *Breathe On Me, Breath of God*
Breathe on me, Breath of God,
Fill me with life anew,
That I may love what thou dost love,
And do what thou wouldst do.

Breathe on me, Breath of God,
Until my heart is pure,
Until with thee I will one will
To do and to endure.

Breathe on me, Breath of God,
Till I am wholly thine,
Until this earthly part of me
Glows with thy fire divine.

Breathe on me, Breath of God,
So shall I never die,
But live with thee the perfect life
Of thine eternity. Amen.

SCRIPTURE READING *(1 Corinthians 13)*
If I speak in the tongues of men and of angels, but have not love, I am
a noisy gong or a clanging cymbal. And if I have prophetic powers,
and understand all mysteries and knowledge, and if I have all faith,
so as to remove mountains, but have not love, I am nothing. If I give
away all I have, and if I deliver my body to be burned, but have not
love, I gain nothing.

Love is patient and kind; love is not jealous or boastful; it is not
arrogant or rude. Love does not insist on its own way; it is not
irritable or resentful; it does not rejoice at wrong, but rejoices in the
right. Love bears all things, believes all things, hopes all things,
endures all things.

Love never ends; as for prophecies, they will pass away; as for
tongues, they will cease; as for knowledge, it will pass away. For our
knowledge is imperfect and our prophecy is imperfect; but when the
perfect comes, the imperfect will pass away. When I was a child, I
spoke like a child, I thought like a child, I reasoned like a child; when
I became a man, I gave up childish ways. For now we see in a mirror
dimly, but then face to face. Now I know in part; then I shall understand fully, even as I have been fully understood. So faith, hope, love
abide, these three; but the greatest of these is love.

AGAPE
*(At a Moravian love feast a large plain sweet roll and hot coffee with
cream and sugar is served to each person. Everyone eats together while
music is played. Begin the music and have servers pass out the rolls and
coffee. When everyone has been served, continue.)*

PRAYER *before eating:*
Our Lord God, we gather in your love. Unite us into *your* community
of faithful people. In gratitude for love received we share in this love
feast ever mindful of your grace which unites us. **Amen.**

*(Eating is conducted in silence; music can be played — Bach's St. Matthew
Passion or B Minor Mass would be appropriate; so would brass music or
Moravian hymns.)*

PRAYER *after eating:*
O Lord, we have eaten together in love. Bless us that we might live
under the judgment and mercy of your Gospel to the end that your
will is done and your community comes. **Amen.**

HYMN: *We've A Story to Tell to the Nations*
We've a story to tell to the nations,
That shall turn our hearts to the right,
A story of truth and mercy,
A story of peace and light,
A story of peace and light.

REFRAIN:
For the darkness shall turn to dawning,
and the dawning to noonday bright,
And Christ's great kingdom shall come on earth,
The kingdom of love and light. Amen.

We've a song to be sung to the nations,
That shall lift our hearts to the Lord,
A song that shall conquer evil
And shatter the spear and sword,
And shatter the spear and sword.
REFRAIN:

We've a message to give to the nations,
That the Lord who reigneth above
Hath sent us his Son to save us,

And show us that God is love,
And show us that God is love.
REFRAIN:

We've a Savior to show to the nations,
Who the path of sorrow hath trod,
That all of the world's great peoples
Might come to the truth of God,
Might come to the truth of God!
REFRAIN:

FAITH SHARING *(Give each person an opportunity to share a testimony of her or his faith.)*

HYMN: *Blest Be the Tie That Binds*
Blest be the tie that binds
Our hearts in Christian love;
The deep communion that we find
Is like to that above.

Before our Maker's throne
We pour our ardent prayers;
Our fears, our hopes, our aims are one,
Our comforts and our cares.

We share each other's woes,
Each other's burdens bear,
And often for each other flows
The sympathizing tear.

When we are called to part
It gives us inward pain,
But we shall still be joined in heart,
And hope to meet again.

KISS OF PEACE *(Share together.)*

HYMN: *Be Thou My Vision*
Be thou my vision, O Lord of my heart;
Nought be all else to me save that thou art.
Thou my best thought, by day or by night,
Waking or sleeping, thy presence my light.

Be thou my wisdom, and thou my true word;
I ever with thee and thou with me, Lord;
Thou my great Father, I thy true child;
Thou in me dwelling, and I with thee one.

Riches I heed not, nor the world's empty praise;
Thou mine inheritance, now and always;
Thou and thou only, first in my heart,
High King of heaven, my treasure thou art.

High King of heaven, my victory won,
May I reach heaven's joys, O bright heaven's Sun!
Heart of my own heart, whatever befall,
Still be my vision, O Ruler of all. Amen.

COMMISSION *(Place a pinch of salt in each person's hand. As they place
it in their mouths say, "Go forth, remember that you are called to be the
salt of the earth.")*

EXERCISE NUMBER TWO: *Exploring the Faith*
After about 60 minutes of silence, gather together.
1. *Share the names of important persons and events in the Bible and
   church history.*
2. *Explain why each is important for you and your understanding of the
   faith.*
3. *Discuss the meaning of each person or event mentioned.*
Follow by a silent walk.

THE SEDER
(Silence is broken; it is time for a joyful meal.)
(All raise cup of wine.)

Blessed art thou, O Lord our God, Ruler of the universe, Creator of the fruit of the vine. Blessed art thou who hast made of one earth, one flesh, all the peoples of the world. Blessed art thou, who hast made all peoples holy and hast commanded us, even against our will, to become a beacon for justice and liberation for them all. Blessed art thou, O Lord God, Ruler of the universe, who didst preserve us and sustain us to reach this season.

(All drink cup of wine. Leader washes his or her hands in silence, then dips greens into salt water and distributes to the others present. When all are served leader says this blessing and all eat:)

Blessed art thou, O Lord our God, Ruler of the universe, Creator of the fruit of the earth.

(Leader breaks the middle matzah, leaving half on the plate and putting half away for after the meal.)

This is the bread that our fathers ate in the land of Egypt. Let anyone who is hungry, come and eat. Let anyone who is needy, come and celebrate the Passover. *(Leader opens door.)* As our door is open, may not only the hungry come but also the spirit of the prophet Elijah that we may think wisely and feel deeply as we celebrate this Passover. For Elijah we set aside this cup of wine.

(Leader puts the plate down, covers matzah, fills the second cup of wine. The youngest present asks the Four Questions:)

Why is this night different from other nights?
On all other nights we eat leavened bread or matzah,
    on this night why only matzah?
On all other nights we eat all kinds of herbs,
    on this night why only bitter herbs?
On all other nights we do not dip our herbs even once,
    on this night why dip twice?
On all other nights we eat in any manner,
    on this night why do we all recline?

(Leader uncovers the matzah and begins the reply:)

Because we were slaves to Pharaoh in Egypt, and the Lord our God brought us out from there with a strong hand and an outstretched arm. Now if God had not brought us out of Egypt, then we and our children would still be slaves. Though we had all wisdom, all understanding, and were all old and learned in the law of God, it would still be our duty to tell the story of the Exodus from Egypt. And this is our story.

Moses lived in a period of dictatorship. Our people were slaves. The bosses made them work under a speed-up system, and committed horrible atrocities, such as trying to kill all the boy-babies born to our people.

Moses himself was saved from such a death only because his mother hid him in a reed basket in the Nile River. There he was found by the daughter of the Pharaoh, which is what they called their dictator in Egypt. The princess took Moses to the royal palace and had him brought up as her son.

When Moses was a young man, he became curious about the Hebrew slaves, and one day went to the brickyards where some of them were working. The first thing he saw was an Egyptian boss hitting a Hebrew laborer. Moses was a powerful young man. He lost his temper. He hit the boss — and killed him! He buried the body hastily in the sand, and went back to the palace.

But a fire was kindled in Moses' heart, a fire of concern about his people and their suffering. The next day he went back to the hot brickyards. Then he learned two things that those who try to help their fellows often discover.

He found, first, that slaves often spend as much time and energy fighting each other as they do fighting their common oppressors, and second, that slaves do not always welcome their deliverers. They get accustomed to being slaves. Even after they have been freed, if freedom brings hardship, they may want to return "to the fleshpots of Egypt."

This time Moses found two Hebrews fighting each other. When he rebuked them, they turned on him and said, "Who made you our boss? Do you mean to kill us as you did that Egyptian yesterday?"

Moses feared that in order to turn suspicion away from themselves they would tell the Egyptians that he had killed the boss. He concluded that it might not be healthy to stay around those parts, so he ran away. He settled down to a nice comfortable life, raising a family and feeding the flocks of his father-in-law.

Only, after a while, God came into the picture. What was the sign that God had come? It was a bush that burned and burned and did not stop burning. Moses had had a fire kindled in his heart once, but it went out, or at least died down. God is the Being whose heart does not stop burning, in whom the flame does not die down.

What was God all burned up about? The voice that came out of the bush said, "I have seen the affliction of my people that are in Egypt and have heard their cry by reason of their oppressors." It was the physical, economic, and spiritual suffering, the injustice, the degradation to which actual people were subjected here on earth that caused God's concern.

And the proof that God had entered into Moses and that Moses had really been "converted" was that he had to go back and identify himself with his enslaved people — "organize them into Brickmakers' Union Number One" — and lead them out of hunger and slavery into freedom and into "a good land, and a large land, a land flowing with milk and honey."

At the head of the Ten Commandments stand these great words: "I am the Lord your God, who brought you out of the land of Egypt, out of the slave-house. You shall have no other gods before me" — before this God who is in the hearts of his prophets as the Eternal Flame; who will not let them rest where there is injustice and inequality until these have been done away with and people set about building God's House instead of the slave-house.

To be religious, our foreparents discovered, is to get out of Egypt into Canaan; to refuse to be slaves or contented draft-horses; to build brotherhood and sisterhood in freedom — because that is what people, the children of God, were created to do! And religious leaders are those who identify themselves with the oppressed, so that men and women may carry out this, their true mission in the world.

(Leader lifts the cup and says:)
Therefore it is our duty to thank and praise, glorify and adore God, who did all these wonders for us, who brought us out of slavery to freedom, from anguish to joy, from mourning to festival, from darkness to light. Praise the Lord!

Blessed art Thou, O Lord our God, Ruler of the universe, who redeemed us and our forefathers from Egypt. Blessed art Thou, O Lord who redeemed Israel. **Blessed art Thou, O Lord our God, Ruler of the universe, Creator of the fruit of the vine.**

SONG: *Let My People Go*
When Israel was in Egypt's land,
      Let my people go.
Oppressed so hard they could not stand,
      Let my people go!

CHORUS:
Go down, Moses,
'Way down in Egypt's land;
Tell ol' Pharaoh,
Let my people go!

(All drink the second cup of wine; leader washes hands and says:)
Blessed art Thou, O Lord our God, Ruler of the universe, who makes us holy with the commandments, and commands us concerning the washing of hands.
      "We've got some difficult days ahead. But it really doesn't matter with me now. Because I've been to the mountaintop. I won't mind. Like anybody, I would like to live a long life. Longevity has its place. But I'm not concerned about that now. I just want to do God's will.

And he's allowed me to go up to the mountain. And I've looked over, and I've seen the Promised Land. I may not get there with you, but I want you to know tonight that we as a people will get to the Promised Land. So I'm happy tonight. I'm not fearing any man. Mine eyes have seen the glory of the coming of the Lord!"—Martin Luther King, Jr.

SONG: *Go, Tell It on the Mountain*
CHORUS:
Go, tell it on the mountain,
Over the hills and everywhere,
Go, tell it on the mountain,
To let my people go!

Who are the children dressed in white?
Let my people go!
Must be the children of the Israelite.
Let my people go!   .
CHORUS:

Who are the children dressed in red?
Let my people go!
Must be the people that Moses led.
Let my people go!
CHORUS:

So the struggles for freedom that remain will be more strange and difficult than any we have met so far. For we must struggle for a freedom that enfolds stern justice, stern bravery, stern love, and simple joy. Blessed art thou, O Lord our God! who hast confronted us with the necessity of choice and of creating our own book of thy Law. How many and how hard are the choices and the tasks the Almighty has set before us!

For if we were to end a single genocide but did not stop the other wars that are killing men and women as we sit here, it would not be sufficient;

If we were to end those bloody wars but did not disarm the nations of the weapons that could destroy all mankind, it would not be sufficient;

If we were to disarm the nations but did not end the pollution and
poisoning of our planet, it would not be sufficient;

If we were to end the poisoning of our planet but did not prevent
some people from wallowing in luxury while others starved, it
would not be sufficient;

If we were to make sure that no one starved but did not end police
brutality in many countries, it would not be sufficient;

If we were to end outright police brutality but did not free the daring
poets from their jails, it would not be sufficient;

If we were to free the poets from their jails but cramped the minds of
people so that they could not understand the poets, it would not
be sufficient;

If we allowed men and women to explore their inner ecstasies but
did not allow them to love one another and share in the human
fraternity, it would not be sufficient.

How much then are we in duty bound to struggle, work, share, give,
think, plan, feel, organize, sit in, speak out, dream, hope, and
be on behalf of humankind! For we must end the genocide, stop
the bloody wars that are killing men and women as we sit here,
disarm the nations of the deadly weapons that threaten to destroy us all, end the poisoning of our planet, make sure that no
one starves, stop police brutality in many countries, free the
poets from their jails, educate us all to understand their poetry,
liberate us all to explore our inner ecstasies, and encourage and
aid us to love one another and share in the human fraternity. All
these!

For, as is said,
". . . they shall beat their swords into plowshares, and their spears
into pruning hooks; nation shall not lift up sword against nation,
neither shall they learn war any more. But they shall sit every man
under his vine and under his fig tree, and none shall make them
afraid, for the mouth of the Lord of hosts has spoken. For we will
walk in the name of the Lord our God for ever and ever."

Blessed art thou, O Lord our God, King of the universe, who has
promised us a world of peace, justice, and freedom. Blessed art thou,
O Lord our God, King of the universe, who dost strengthen us to

build that world! Blessed art thou, O Lord our God, King of the universe, who strengthened our forefathers to win their liberty and fulfill thy promise to end the captivity in Egypt.

Not only in song and story must we remember their struggle, but in the very food that we fuse with our bodies tonight. Whosoever does not make mention of the three things used on the Passover has not done his duty; and these are they: the paschal lamb, the unleavened cake, and bitter herb.

(Leader raises the lamb and says:)
The paschal lamb, which our ancestors ate during the existence of the Holy Temple, what did it denote? It denoted that the Most Holy, blessed be he, passed over our fathers' houses in Egypt; as is said, "You shall say, 'It is the sacrifice of the Lord's Passover, for he passed over the houses of the people of Israel in Egypt, when he slew the Egyptians but spared our houses.' And the people bowed their heads and worshiped."

(Leader takes hold of the matzah, shows it to the company, and says:)
These unleavened cakes, wherefore do we eat them? Because there was not sufficient time for the dough of our ancestors to leaven, before the Holy Supreme King of Kings, blessed be he, appeared unto them, and redeemed them; as is said, "And they baked unleavened cakes of the dough which they had brought out of Egypt; for it was not leavened, because they were thrust out of Egypt and could not tarry, neither had they made any provision for themselves."

(Leader takes hold of the bitter herbs, shows them to the company, and says:)
This bitter herb, wherefore do we eat it? Because the Egyptians embittered the lives of our ancestors in Egypt; as is said, " . . . and [they] made their lives bitter with cruel bondage, in mortar and brick, and in all kinds of work in the field; in all their work they made them serve with rigor."

It therefore is incumbent on every person in every generation — not merely every Jew, but every man and woman — to look upon himself, as if he had actually gone forth from Egypt! As it is said, "And you shall tell your son, on that day, 'It is because of what the Lord did for me when I came out of Egypt.' " It was not our ancestors only that the Most Holy, blessed be he, redeemed from Egypt, but us also did He redeem with them, as is said, " . . . and he brought us out from there, that he might bring us in and give us the land which he swore to give to our fathers."

(Leader covers the matzah, takes the cup of wine in his or her hand, and says:)
We therefore are in duty bound to thank, praise, adore, glorify, extol, honor, bless, exalt, and reverence him who wrought all the miracles for our ancestors and us: for he brought us forth from bondage to freedom, from sorrow to joy, from mourning into holy days, from darkness to great light, and from servitude to redemption: and therefore let us chant unto him a new song, hallelujah!

(Leader holds up the matzah and says:)
Blessed art thou, O Lord our God, Ruler of the universe, who brings forth bread from the earth. Blessed art thou who makes us holy with the commandments, and commanded us concerning the eating of matzah.

(Leader breaks the matzah, distributes it to those present, and all eat it together. It was at this point that Jesus instituted the Holy Communion by saying to his disciples, "Take, eat, this is my Body which is given for you; do this in remembrance of me.")

(All pass and eat bitter herbs [salt water, parsley, and horseradish] together; leader says:)

Blessed art thou, O Lord our God, Ruler of the universe, who makes us holy with the commandments, and commanded us concerning the eating of bitter herbs.

(All pass naroset [combination of cinnamon, crushed nuts, and apple] and a small piece of matzah, make a sandwich of them, and eat.)

In remembrance of the Temple, we do as Rabbi Hillel did in Temple times; he put matzah and bitter herbs together to observe the command, "They shall eat it with matzah and bitter herbs."

(Leader fills the third cup of wine.)

Let us bless the Lord.
May the name of the Lord be blessed now and forever.

Let us praise our God, whose food we have eaten.
Blessed be our God whose food we have eaten and in whose goodness we live.

Blessed art thou, O Lord our God, Ruler of the universe, who sustains the whole universe with goodness, grace, loving kindness, and mercy, who provides food for all. We thank you, O Lord our God, for the good land you gave our fathers, and for bringing us out of the land of Egypt. Have mercy, Lord, on Israel your people, and Jerusalem your city, on the royal house of David your anointed, and on the holy Temple called by your name. O God our Father, be a shepherd to us, pasture us, feed us, sustain and support us, and give us relief from all our afflictions. O build up Jerusalem, the holy city, in our day! Blessed art thou, O God, who dost build up Jerusalem. **Amen.**

Blessed art thou, O Lord our God, Ruler of the universe, Creator of the fruit of the vine.

(It was at this point that Our Lord Jesus Christ took the cup and gave it to the disciples, saying, "Drink ye all of this, for this is my Blood of the new covenant, which is shed for you, and for all, for the forgiveness of sins. Do this, as often as ye drink it, in remembrance of me."
(All drink the third cup; leader refills the cups.)

Pour out thy mercy on the nations that know thee not, and upon the kingdoms that call not upon thy name. Forgive them for consuming Jacob and laying waste his habitation. Pour out thy mercy on them and let thy loving kindness overtake them. Pursue them in love and bring them into the peace of heaven.

SELECTIONS FROM THE HILLEL PSALMS:
Give thanks to the Lord, for he is good;
For his love endures forever

Let Israel now proclaim;
For his love endures forever.

Let all who love the Lord now proclaim;
His love endures forever.

The stone which the builders rejected
Is become the chief cornerstone.

This is the Lord's doing,
And it is marvelous in our eyes.

Save us, Lord, we pray you.
O Lord grant us deliverance.

Blessed art thou, O Lord our God, Ruler of the universe, Creator of the fruit of the vine. The Passover meal is over; we have kept it according to custom and law. God grant we may so keep it time and again. O Lord of heaven above, restore your people Israel in your love, and lead your redeemed people to Zion in joy.

(All drink the fourth cup.)

SONG: *Shalom*

EXERCISE NUMBER THREE: *Body Time*
Work and play. Silence is broken. Engage in some activity alone or with one or more persons that will make a positive contribution to the improvement of your environment.

End with a period of 15-30 minutes of silent meditation in preparation for worship.

CELEBRATION OF CHRIST'S WITNESSES

INTRODUCTION
Rejoice in the Lord, you righteous!
Sing for joy, all upright hearts!
Heaven, blaze in gladness,
And all you saints, apostles, prophets!

Lord, I stand before you,
You have taken my hand;
You will lead me by your counsel,
And then bring me into glory.

Whom could I count on beside you?
With you I desire nothing more on the earth.
My heart and my flesh are burned up,
Rock of my heart, God, my portion forever!

Coming to God is my wealth,
I have taken the Lord for my refuge;
So I will tell all your works,
At the gates of the daughter of Zion.

SCRIPTURE READING *(Ecclesiasticus 15:11-20)*
Do not say, "The Lord is to blame for my failure";
it is for you to avoid doing what he hates.
Do not say, "It was he who led me astray";
he has no use for sinful men.
The Lord hates every kind of vice;
you cannot love it and still fear him.
When he made man in the beginning,
he left him free to make his own decisions;
if you choose, you can keep the commandments;
whether or not you keep faith is yours to decide.
He has set before you fire and water;
reach out and take which you choose;
before man lie life and death,

and whichever he prefers is his.
For in his great wisdom and mighty power
the Lord sees everything.
He keeps watch over those who fear him;
no human act escapes his notice.
But he has commanded no man to be wicked,
nor has he given license to commit sin.

The righteous rejoice in the presence of God.
They exult and they dance for joy!
The righteous rejoice in the presence of God.

To the Lord our God belong the secrets of life.
They exult and they dance for joy!
The righteous rejoice in the presence of God.

HYMN: *For All the Saints*
For all the saints, who from their labors rest,
Who thee by faith, before the world confessed,
Thy name, most holy, be forever blessed.
Alleluia, Alleluia!

Thou wast their Rock, their Shelter, and their Might;
Their strength and solace in the well-fought fight;
Thou in the darkness drear, their one true light.
Alleluia, Alleluia!

O blest communion of the saints divine,
We live and struggle, they in glory shine;
Yet all are one in Thee, for all are Thine.
Alleluia, Alleluia!

And when the strife is fierce, the struggle long,
Steals on the ear the distant freedom song,
And hearts are brave again, and arms are strong.
Alleluia, Alleluia!

INTERCESSIONS
Lord have mercy,
Christ have mercy.

Lord have mercy,
Christ hear us.

God the Creator of heaven and earth,
Mercy for us!

God the Son, Redeemer and Liberator of the world,
Mercy for us!

God the Holy Spirit, Sustainer and Advocate of us all,
Mercy for us!

God, one God, thrice holy,
Mercy for us!

With the angels, the archangels and the spirits of the blessed, Lord,
we praise you!
Glory! Lord of life!

With the prophets, Lord, we bless you!
Glory! Lord of life!

With the apostles and the evangelists, Lord, we give you thanks!
Glory! Lord of life!

With all Christ's martyrs, Lord, we offer you our bodies in sacrifice!
Glory! Lord of life!

With all the saints, witnesses to the Gospel, Lord, we consecrate our
lives!
Glory! Lord of life!

With all the faithful of the church, Lord, we adore you!
Glory! Lord of life!

Happy the dead who die in the Lord: now they shall rest from their labors, for their works go with them.
Glory! Lord of life!

The Lord be with you,
And with your spirit.
Let us pray.

(Encourage the people to offer their own prayers.)

GENERAL COLLECT
O thou who art the light of the minds that know thee, the life of the souls that love thee, and the strength of the wills that serve thee: help us so to know thee that we may perfectly love thee, and so to love thee that we may truly serve thee, whose service is perfect freedom. Through Jesus Christ our Lord. Amen.

All Holy God, of your infinite goodness, set us aflame with that fire of the Spirit Christ brought upon earth ablaze. **Amen.**

All loving God, there is no greater love than to give our lives for our friends. Grant us such courage that in the company of your martyrs we may at last gaze with joy upon the face of Christ, and find in his glory the crown of your eternal life. **Amen.**

All present and God, you manifested your love in such signs of grace, that Mary sang and rejoiced in your Spirit. Grant us such obedient hearts, that we like Mary may believe in your Word, and be gladdened by the gift of your Son, Jesus Christ, our Lord. **Amen.**

All powerful God, break the power of darkness, let your glory appear among us and make us sharers of your eternity, with all your saints, through Jesus Christ, our Lord. **Amen.**

THE LORD'S PRAYER

HYMN: *Immortal, Invisible, God Only Wise*
Immortal, invisible, God only wise,

In light inaccessible hid from our eyes,
Most blessed, most glorious, the Ancient of Days,
Almighty, victorious, thy great name we praise.

Unresting, unhasting, and silent as light,
Nor wanting, nor wasting, Thou rulest in might;
Thy justice like mountains high soaring above,
Thy clouds which are fountains of goodness and love.

To all, life Thou givest, to both great and small;
In all life Thou livest, the true light of all;
We blossom and flourish as leaves on the tree,
And wither and perish, but naught changeth Thee.

Thou dwellest in glory, thou reignest in light;
Thine angels adore Thee, all veiling their sight;
All praise we would render; O help us to see
'Tis only the splendor of light hideth Thee!

HYMN OF JOB *(Job 42:1-5)*
    Then Job answered the LORD: "I know that thou canst do all
things, and that no purpose of thine can be thwarted.
    'Who is this that hides counsel without knowledge?'
    Therefore I have uttered what I did not understand, things too
wonderful for me, which I did not know.
    'Hear, and I will speak; I will question you, and you declare to me.'
    I had heard of thee by the hearing of the ear, but now my eye sees
thee. . ."

HYMN: *O God, Our Help in Ages Past*
O God, our help in ages past,
Our hope for years to come,
Our shelter from the stormy blast
And our eternal home.

Before the hills in order stood,
Or earth received a frame,
From everlasting thou art God
To endless years the same.

A thousand ages in thy sight
Are like an evening gone,
Short as the watch that ends the night
Before the rising sun.

Time like an ever-rolling stream
Bears mortals all away;
They fly, forgotten, as a dream
Dies at the opening day.

Our God, our help in ages past,
Our hope for years to come,
Be thou our guide while life shall last
And our eternal home.

SONG OF MIRIAM *(Exodus 15:20-21)*
Then Miriam, the prophetess, the sister of Aaron , took a timbrel in
her hand; and all the women went out after her with timbrels and
dancing. And Miriam sang to them:
    "Sing to the Lord, for he has triumphed gloriously;
    the horse and his rider he has thrown into the sea."

HYMN: *Now Thank We All Our God*
Now thank we all our God,
With heart and hands and voices,
Who wondrous things hath done,
In whom this world rejoices,
Who from our mothers' arms,
Hath blessed us on our way,
With countless gifts of love,
And still is ours today.

O may this bounteous God,
Through all our life be near us,
With ever joyful hearts,
And blessed peace to cheer us,
And keep us still in grace,
And guide us when perplexed,

And free us from all ills
In this world and the next.

All praise and thanks to God,
The Source and Ground of Being,
The Christ and Holy Ghost,
Who were from the beginning,
The one eternal God,
Whom earth and heaven adore,
For thus it was, and is now,
And shall be evermore.

SONG OF HANNAH *(1 Samuel 1:2-8)*

"He had two wives; the name of the one was Hannah, and the name
of the other Peninnah. And Peninnah had children, but Hannah had
no children.

Now this man used to go up year by year from his city to worship
and to sacrifice to the LORD of hosts at Shiloh, where the two sons of
Eli, Hophni and Phinehas, were priests of the LORD. On the day
when Elkanah sacrificed, he would give portions to Peninnah his
wife and to all her sons and daughters; and, although he loved Hannah, he would give Hannah only one portion, because the LORD had
closed her womb. And her rival used to provoke her sorely, to irritate
her, because the LORD had closed her womb. So it went on year by
year; as often as she went up to the house of the LORD, she used to
provoke her. Therefore Hannah wept and would not eat. And Elkanah, her husband, said to her, "Hannah, why do you weep? And
why do you not eat? And why is your heart sad? Am I not more to you
than ten sons?"

HYMN: *The Voice of God Is Calling*
The voice of God is calling
Its summons unto us;
As once he spake in Zion,
So now he speaks again:
Whom shall I send to succor
My people in their need?
Whom shall I send to loosen
The bonds of shame and greed?

I hear my people crying
In cot and mine and slum;
No field or mart is silent,
No city street is dumb.
I see my people falling
In darkness and despair.
Whom shall I send to shatter
The fetters which they bear?

We heed, O Lord, thy summons,
And answer: Here are we!
Send us upon thine errand;
Let us thy servants be.
Our strength is dust and ashes,
Our years a passing hour,
But thou canst use our weakness
To magnify thy power.

From ease and plenty save us;
From pride of place absolve;
Purge us of low desire;
Lift us to high resolve;
Take us, and make us holy;
Teach us thy will and way.
Speak, and, behold! we answer;
Command, and we obey!

SONG OF MARY (Luke 1:46-53)

And Mary said, "My soul magnifies the Lord, and my spirit rejoices in God my Savior, for he has regarded the low estate of his handmaiden.

"For behold, henceforth all generations will call me blessed; for he who is mighty has done great things for me, and holy is his name. And his mercy is on those who fear him from generation to generation. He has shown strength with his arm, he has scattered the proud in the imagination of their hearts, he has put down the mighty from their thrones, and exalted those of low degree; he has filled the hungry with good things, and the rich he has sent empty away."

HYMN: *God Rest You Joyful People All*

God rest you joyful people all,
Let nothing you dismay,
Remember Christ, our Saviour,
Was born on Christmas Day,
To show us all the grace of God
When we were gone astray.

REFRAIN:
O tidings of comfort and joy,
comfort and joy,
O tidings of comfort and joy!

From God, who loved us from our birth,
A blessed angel came;
And unto certain shepherds
Brought tidings of the same:
How that in Bethlehem was born
Our hope, the Christ by name.
REFRAIN:

"Fear not, then," said the angel,
"Let nothing you affright;
This day is born a Saviour,
This world's one shining light,
To free all people of the earth
And end this darkest night."
REFRAIN:

Now to our God sing praises,
All you within this place,
And with true love among you all
Each other now embrace;
This holy tide of Christmas
Doth bring redeeming grace.
REFRAIN:

SONG OF SIMEON *(Luke 2:25-32)*

Now there was a man in Jerusalem, whose name was Simeon, and this man was righteous and devout, looking for the consolation of Israel, and the Holy Spirit was upon him. And it had been revealed to him by the Holy Spirit that he should not see death before he had seen the Lord's Christ. And inspired by the Spirit he came into the temple; and when the parents brought in the child Jesus, to do for him according to the custom of the law, he took him up in his arms and blessed God and said, "Lord, now lettest thou thy servant depart in peace, according to thy word; for mine eyes have seen thy salvation which thou hast prepared in the presence of all peoples, a light for revelation to the Gentiles, and for glory to thy people Israel."

HYMN: *Joy to the World! The Lord Is Come*

Joy to the world! the Lord is come:
Let us receive our King;
Let every heart prepare him room,
And heaven and nature sing,
And heaven and nature sing,
And heaven, and heaven and nature sing.

Joy to the earth! the Savior reigns:
Let us our songs employ;
While fields and floods, rocks, hills, and plains
Repeat the sounding joy,
Repeat the sounding joy,
Repeat, repeat the sounding joy.

He rules the world with truth and grace,
And makes the nations prove
The glories of his righteousness,
And wonders of his love,
And wonders of his love,
And wonders, wonders of his love.

SONG OF ZECHARIAH *(Zechariah 9:9-10)*

Rejoice greatly, O daughter of Zion! Shout aloud, O daughter of Jerusalem!

Lo, your king comes to you; triumphant and victorious is he, humble and riding on an ass, on a colt the foal of an ass.

I will cut off the chariot from Ephraim and the war horse from Jerusalem; and the battle bow shall be cut off, and he shall command peace to the nations; his dominion shall be from sea to sea, and from the River to the ends of the earth.

HYMN: *The God of Abraham Praise*
The God of Abraham praise,
All praised be God's name,
Who was, and is, and is to be,
For aye the same!
The one eternal God,
Ere aught that now appears;
The First, the Last: beyond all thought
God's timeless years!

God's spirit floweth free,
High surging where it will;
In prophet's word God spoke of old
God speaketh still.
Established is God's law,
And changeless it shall stand,
Deep writ upon the human heart,
On sea, or land.

God hath eternal life
Implanted in the soul;
God's love shall be our strength and stay,
While ages roll.
Praise to the living God!
All praised be God's name
Who was, and is, and is to be,
For aye the same!
Amen.

SONG OF THE FIRSTBORN *(Luke 4:14-21)*
And Jesus returned in the power of the Spirit into Galilee, and a

report concerning him went out through all the surrounding country. And he taught in their synagogues, being glorified by all.

And he came to Nazareth, where he had been brought up; and he went to the synagogue, as his custom was, on the sabbath day. And he stood up to read; and there was given to him the book of the prophet Isaiah. He opened the book and found the place where it was written,

"The Spirit of the Lord is upon me, because he has anointed me to preach good news to the poor. He has sent me to proclaim release to the captives and recovering of sight to the blind, to set at liberty those who are oppressed, to proclaim the acceptable year of the Lord."

And he closed the book, and gave it back to the attendant, and sat down; and the eyes of all in the synagogue were fixed on him. And he began to say to them, "Today this scripture has been fulfilled in your hearing."

HYMN: *Lead On, O Cloud Of Yahweh*
Lead on, O cloud of Yahweh,
The Exodus is come;
In wilderness and desert
Our tribe shall make its home.
Our slav'ry left behind us,
A vision in us grows,
We seek the land of promise
Where milk and honey flows.

Lead on, O fiery pillar,
We follow yet with fears,
But we shall come rejoicing
Though joy be born of tears;
We are not lost, though wandering,
For by your light we come,
And we are still God's people,
The journey is our home.

Lead on, O God of freedom,
Our guiding spirit be;
Though those who start the journey

The promise may not see,
We pray our sons and daughters
May live to see that land
Where justice rules with mercy
And love is law's demand.

SONG OF THE SPIRIT *(Luke 19:36-38)*
And as he rode along, they spread their garments on the road. As he
was now drawing near, at the descent of the Mount of Olives, the
whole multitude of the disciples began to rejoice and praise God with
a loud voice for all the mighty works that they had seen, saying,
"Blessed is the King who comes in the name of the Lord! Peace in
heaven and glory in the highest!"

HYMN: *All Glory, Laud, and Honor*
All glory, laud, and honor
    To thee, Redeemer, King,
To whom the lips of children
    Made sweet hosannas ring!
The people of the Hebrews
    With palms before thee went;
Our praise and prayer and anthems
    Before thee we present.

Thou art the King of Israel,
    Thou David's royal son,
Who in the Lord's name comest,
    The King and blessed One;
To thee, before thy passion,
    They sang their hymns of praise;
To thee, now high exalted,
    Our melody we raise.

Thou didst accept their praises;
    Accept the prayers we bring,
Who in all good delightest,
    Thou good and gracious King.
All glory, laud, and honor

To thee, Redeemer, King,
To whom the lips of children
    Made sweet hosannas ring!
Amen.

RESPONSE
Come, Holy Spirit,
Inflame our waiting hearts!
Burn us with your love,
Renew us in your life.

Send forth your Spirit, Lord,
Renew the face of the earth.
Creator Spirit, come,
Inflame our waiting hearts.
Your Spirit fills the world,
And knows our every word.

Glory to God
Now and for evermore.
You are, you were, you come.

Happy the poor in heart, the kingdom of heaven is theirs.
Happy the gentle, they will share in the Promised Land.
Happy all who weep, they will be comforted.
Happy are the hungry and thirsty for justice, they will be filled.
Happy the merciful, mercy will be theirs.
Happy the clear in heart, they will see God.
Happy the creators of peace, they will be called sons of God.
Happy all who are persecuted for what is right, the kingdom of
    heaven is theirs.
Happy are you, if they persecute you, if they slander you because of
    Christ: be glad and leap for joy, for your reward in heaven is
    great!

BLESSING
Bless us, Lord, and keep us in the spirit of the Beatitudes. **Amen.**

EXERCISE NUMBER FOUR: *Searching the Word*
Gather for a two-hour community Bible study. Silently read Acts 2-4, then discuss the following sections:

Empowering (Acts 2)
Doing (Acts 3:1-10)
Telling (Acts 3:11-16)
Calling (Acts 3:17-26)
Challenging (Acts 4:1-12)
Growing (Acts 4:13-22)
Being (Acts 4:23-37)

Reflect together on the life of the Christian and the church.

Consider: Was it not an act of God that established the church? Is not the church more than a human voluntary association? Are we not set apart in the church to witness to the Gospel?

Consider: Was not the first evangelistic deed an act of liberation? Does not the Christian act first and thereby witness to the Gospel? Does talk and explanation come later so as to explain the reasons for one's radical deed? Isn't the Christian invitation to join in such radical actions?

Consider: When we truly live out the Gospel, do we not usually so disrupt the social order that we are considered troublemakers? Is not there a price for living the Gospel?

Consider: What sort of community is the church? Is it not a community radically different from any other? Does it not witness in its life to an alternative?

Ask: How much is the spirit alive in our congregation? In our lives?
    What actions are we performing that witness to the transforming power of the Gospel in the world?
    How do we explain to our community why we act as we do?
    To what do we call people when we invite them to church?
    What price has our congregation paid for its witness to the Gospel?

What sort of growth have we witnessed in the last year?
What sort of alternative to life do we offer through the life of our congregation?

A SERVICE FROM THE THIRD WORLD

INVITATION
The spirit of the Lord is upon me because the Lord has anointed me.
He has sent me to announce good news to the poor,
to proclaim release for prisoners and recovery of sight for the blind,
to let the broken victims go free,
to proclaim the year of the Lord's favor.
Today, in our hearing, this text has come true.

LITANY
The old order is passing away; your new order, Lord, has already begun, and we are numbered among its signs. Through your Spirit in our hearts you have set us free.
You have called us out of darkness into your marvelous light.
You have opened our eyes, given us hope that we shall live in the glorious liberty of the children of God. But not alone, Lord; not while others remain poor, brokenhearted, imprisoned, blind, and bruised.
You have called us out of darkness into your marvelous light.
So, Lord, we pray for our brothers and sisters, your family oppressed by ignorance and poverty, caught in a web of injustice and apathy, cut off from one another by language, culture, color, class, and creed.
You have called them out of darkness into your marvelous light.
Through education may the powerless be led to self-discovery, the despised find new dignity, the dispossessed be enabled to claim their place in the community of free people.
You have called them out of darkness into your marvelous light.
Give to your church a vision of the total liberation of humanity. Grant us the wisdom to hear the voice of the foolish and the strength of the weak, that through those who are nothing we may understand the Word of Christ.
You are calling us out of darkness into your marvelous light.
But we tend to love darkness rather than light. We shrink from the

responsibility of freedom, the uncertainty of the desert, the conflict of the Cross. We keep turning back, preferring the security of slavery to the adventure of the Promised Land.

Call us out of darkness into your marvelous light.

Call us, Lord Jesus Christ, that we may follow. May we follow you not only as one who goes ahead, but as one who journeys with us: Lord Jesus Christ, freeing us, uniting us!

Let us be content to learn the meaning of your way as we walk in it. **Amen.**

SCRIPTURE *(Acts 3:6-10)*

But Peter said, "I have no silver and gold, but I give you what I have; in the name of Jesus Christ of Nazareth, walk." And he took him by the right hand and raised him up; and immediately his feet and ankles were made strong. And leaping up he stood and walked and entered the temple with them, walking and leaping and praising God. And all the people saw him walking and praising God, and recognized him as the one who sat for alms at the Beautiful Gate of the temple; and they were filled with wonder and amazement at what had happened to him.

SILENT MEDITATION

CONFESSING CHRIST

Who are we, Lord, that we should confess you?

We can hardly speak for ourselves; how could we speak in your name?

We believe in your Word but our minds are often full of doubt.

We trust your promises but our hearts are often fearful.

Captivate our minds, Lord, and let your Spirit dwell in our hearts that we may feel and taste your love.

For necessity is laid upon us; woe to us if we do not preach the Gospel.

How can we call new disciples for you, Lord, while our community, your church, is divided and all too conformed to the pattern of this world? We preach your power of love while we succumb, like all others, to the love of power. We proclaim your justice while we remain caught up in structures of injustice.

Awaken in us the spirit of unity
that we may feel the pain of your Body divided,
and yearn and reach out for fuller union with you
and among ourselves.
Inflame us with the power of your love,
that it may consume the vanity of power.
Make us hunger and thirst for justice,
that our words may be given authority as signs of your
     justice.
**For necessity is laid upon us; woe to us if we do not preach the
     Gospel.**
How can we sing your song, O Lord, in a strange land?
How can we witness to your all-embracing love with lives full of
     painful contradictions?
How can we be ambassadors of reconciliation in a world enslaved by
     sin and death;
where children suffer and starve, and many labor in vain while a few
     live in luxury;
where in the midst of our lives we dwell under the shadow of death?
What shall we say to our own hearts when they cry from the depths:
     "Where is now your God?"
**For necessity is laid upon us; woe to us if we do not preach the
     Gospel.**
God, mysterious and hidden,
you keep us captive while you are the open door,
you make us suffer while your suffering heals us,
you lead us into the depths of despair while the
morning star of hope is shining above us.
Lord crucified, Lord risen: come, transform the
necessities that are laid upon us into freedom
and grant us the courage to do your Word.
Lord, we believe—help our unbelief.
**For necessity is laid upon us; woe to us if we do not preach the
     Gospel.**

PRAYER RESPONSE
SONG: *Kum Ba Yah*
(All sing:) **Someone's crying, Lord, kum ba yah.**
Someone's crying, Lord, somewhere.

Some is millions, somewhere is many places.
There are tears of suffering,
There are tears of weakness and disappointment,
There are tears of strength and resistance,
There are the tears of the rich, and the tears of the poor.

Someone's crying, Lord, redeem the times.

(All sing:) **Someone's dying, Lord, kum ba yah.**
Some are dying of hunger and thirst,
Someone is dying because somebody else is enjoying
Too many unnecessary and superfluous things.
Someone is dying because people go on exploiting one another.
Some are dying because there are structures and systems
That crush the poor and alienate the rich.
Someone's dying, Lord,
Because we are still not prepared to take sides,
To make a choice, to be a witness.

Someone's dying, Lord, redeem the times.

(All sing:) **Someone's shouting, Lord, kum ba yah.**
Someone's shouting out loudly and clearly.
Someone has made a choice.
Someone is ready to stand up against the times.
Someone is shouting out,
Offering her very existence in love and anger
To fight death surrounding us,
To wrestle with the evils with which we crucify each other.

Someone's shouting, Lord, redeem the times.

(All sing:) **Someone's praying, Lord, kum ba yah.**
Someone's praying, Lord.
We are praying in tears and anger,
In frustration and weakness,
In strength and endurance.
We are shouting and wrestling,
As Jacob wrestled with the angel.

And was touched,
And was marked,
And became a blessing.

We are praying, Lord.
Spur our imagination,
Sharpen our political will.

Through Jesus Christ you have let us know where you want us to be.
Help us to be there now;
Be with us, touch us, mark us, let us be a blessing,
Let your power be present in our weakness.

Someone's praying, Lord, redeem the times.

(All sing:) **Someone's praying, Lord, kum ba yah.**

INTERCESSORY PRAYERS *(Encourage people to pray their own prayers.)*

SILENCE

BENEDICTION
Bless us, O Lord, our judge and redeemer, with the wisdom and passion to struggle with your Word. Send us forth with open minds and hearts to know your will.
Amen.

EXERCISE NUMBER FIVE: *Living the Word*
("Only the one who obeys can believe"—Bonhoeffer.)

Silently meditate on Acts 3:1-10.

Answer the following questions as specifically as possible:

Who are the lame that lie outside your gates today?
Who are the broken in the world outside the doors of the church?

Whose wounds cry out for healing on the Jericho roads that run through
   your community?
Who are the prisoners, the hungry, the blind, the captive, and the oppressed in the world?

Then:

Do we walk by the lame? When?
Are we content to give alms to the hurt? When?
Do we accept limits and say that nothing can be done? When?
Do we act as if this were the best of all worlds? When?

Describe as specifically as possible:

What miracles can God perform through us?
What sights and wonders of God's coming community need to be brought
   to pass where we live?
What would it mean for me to join God in healing the hurts, releasing the
   captives, liberating the oppressed, and empowering the helpless in my
   daily life?
What can I do to bring Good News to those who only know the bad news
   of the 6:00 P.M. report?

Be accountable (about an hour before worship):

Share your struggles with one another.
Minister to one another. Help one another work through your understandings, sorrows, and callings. Strive to arrive at a sense of a proper
   social respone to the needy in your midst.

Use the last 15 minutes for silent meditation before coming to worship in
   silence.

BAPTISMAL RENEWAL

INTRODUCTION
Light and peace, in Jesus Christ our Lord.
Thanks be to God.

Jesus said, "You are the light of the world. A city built on a hill cannot be hid. No one lights a lamp to put it under a bucket, but on a lamp-stand where it gives light for everyone in the house. And you, like the lamp, must shed light among your fellow men, so that they may see the good you do, and give glory to your Father in heaven."

The apostle Paul said, "It is not ourselves that we proclaim; we proclaim Christ Jesus as Lord, and ourselves as your servants, for Jesus' sake. For the same God who said, 'Out of darkness let light shine,' has caused his light to shine within us, to give the light of revelation—the revelation of the glory of God in the face of Jesus Christ."

Will you proclaim by word and example the Good News of God in Christ?
I will, with God's help.

Will you seek and serve Christ in all persons, loving your neighbor as yourself?
I will, with God's help.

Will you strive for justice and peace among all people, and respect the dignity of every human being?
I will, with God's help.

THANKSGIVING OVER THE WATER
(Pour water into a large bowl.)
We thank you, Almighty God, for the gift of water. Over it the Holy Spirit moved in the beginning of creation. Through it you led the children of Israel out of their bondage in Egypt into the land of promise. In it your Son Jesus received the baptism of John and was anointed by the Holy Spirit as the Messiah, the Christ, to lead us, through his death and resurrection, from the bondage of sin into everlasting life.

We thank you, God, for the water of baptism. In it we are buried with Christ in his death. By it we share in his resurrection. Through it we are reborn by the Holy Spirit.

Now sanctify this water, we pray you, by the power of your Holy Spirit, that we might be reminded of our baptism and renewed in our faith.

To him, to you, and to the Holy Spirit, be all honor and glory, now and for ever. Amen.

(Encourage persons in silence to come forward, place their hand in the water, and make some sign of devotion, saying: "I, [name], have been baptized. Bless me that I might be faithful.")

PRAYERS
The Lord be with you.
And also with you.
Let us pray.

Deliver us, O Lord, from the way of sin and death.
Lord, hear our prayer.

Open our hearts to your grace and truth.
Lord, hear our prayer.

Fill us with your holy and life-giving Spirit.
Lord, hear our prayer.

Keep us in the faith and communion of your holy church.
Lord, hear our prayer.

Teach us to love others in the power of the Spirit.
Lord, hear our prayer.

Send us into the world in witness to your love.
Lord, hear our prayer.

Bring us to the fullness of your peace and glory.
Lord, hear our prayer.

Grant, O Lord, that all who are baptized into the death of Jesus Christ

your Son may live in the power of his resurrection and look for him to
come again in glory; who lives and reigns now and forever. **Amen.**

Almighty God, we thank you that by the death and resurrection of
your Son Jesus Christ you have overcome sin and brought us to
yourself, and that by the sealing of your Holy Spirit you have bound
us to your service. Renew in us your servants the covenant you made
with us at our baptism. Send us forth in the power of that Spirit to
perform the service you set before us; through Jesus Christ your Son
our Lord, who lives and reigns with you and the Holy Spirit, one
God, now and forever. **Amen.**

Our father in heaven,
    hallowed be your name,
    your kingdom come,
    your will be done,
    on earth as in heaven.
Give us today our daily bread.
Forgive us our sins,
    as we forgive those
        who sin against us.
Save us from the time of trial
    and deliver us from evil.
For the kingdom, the power,
    and the glory are yours,
    now and forever. Amen.

All praise and thanks to you, most merciful God, for adopting us as
your own children, for incorporating us into your holy church, and
for making us worthy to share in the inheritance of the saints in light;
through Jesus Christ your Son our Lord, who lives and reigns with
you and the Holy Spirit, one God, forever and ever. **Amen.**

**Almighty, everlasting God, let our prayer in your sight be as in-
cense, the lifting up of our hands as the evening sacrifice. Give us
grace to recognize you in the lives of those around us. Stir up in us
the flame of that love which burned in the heart of your son as he
bore his passion, and let it burn in us to eternal life and to the ages of
ages. Amen.**

The Lord bless you and keep you. **Amen.**
The Lord make his face to shine upon you
   and be gracious to you. **Amen.**
The Lord lift up his countenance upon you
   and give you peace. **Amen.**

Thanks be to God.

PRAYERS FOR THE WORLD
(optional)

INTRODUCTION
Blessed be our God for all time,
now and forevermore.
Amen.

O come, let me fall down and worship.
O come, let us fall down and worship Christ, our God.

O come, let me fall down and worship Christ among us.
**Holy God, holy and mighty, holy and immortal,
have mercy upon us.**

Out of the depths I cry to thee,
Lord, hear my voice!
**O let thine ears be attentive
to the voice of our pleading.**

If thou, O Lord, shouldst mark my guilt,
Lord, how can I survive?
**But with thee is found forgiveness:
For this we revere thee.**

EPISTLE *(James 2:14-20)*
What does it profit, my brethren, if a man says he has faith but has
not works? Can his faith save him? If a brother or sister is ill-clad and
in lack of daily food, and one of you says to them, "Go in peace, be
warmed and filled," without giving them the things needed for the
body, what does it profit? So faith by itself, if it has no works, is dead.

But some one will say, "You have faith and I have works." Show me your faith apart from your works, and I by my works will show you my faith. You believe that God is one; you do well. Even the demons believe—and shudder.

RESPONSORY
Heal my soul for I have sinned against thee.
Heal my soul for I have sinned against thee.
I have said: Lord, have mercy on me!
For I have sinned against thee.
Glory be to the Creator, and to the Redeemer, and to the Sustainer.
Heal my soul for I have sinned against thee.

SILENT MEDITATION

VERSICLES
Christ loves us and has freed us from our sins with his life's blood.
He made of us a royal house, to serve as the ministers of his God and ours.

PRAYERS
Beloved brothers and sisters, remembering Christ's passion, when, from the height of the cross, he stretched out his arms over the universe, let us pray for all people throughout the world.
Let us pray to the Lord.
For the holy church of God, that the Lord may grant it everywhere peace and unity, to the glory of God almighty,
Let us pray to the Lord.
Almighty and everliving God, who didst manifest in Christ thy glory to all nations, keep the Church in thy love: may it extend throughout the world and persevere in the faith.
O Lord, hear us and have mercy.
For all bishops and pastors, for all ministers and the whole people of God,
Let us pray to the Lord.
Almighty and everliving God, whose Spirit sanctifies and guides the church, we pray unto thee for all the members of thy Body: may every one in their place serve thee faithfully.

O Lord, hear us and have mercy.
For all who are approaching the light, that the Lord may open their hearts and integrate them by baptism into the Body of his Son,
Let us pray to the Lord.
Almighty and everliving God, who always callest new children into thy church, increase their insight and their faith: may they be born again at the source of baptism and be counted among thine adopted children.
O Lord, hear us and have mercy.
For all throughout the world, who live in misery, loneliness, sickness, famine, captivity and persecution,
Let us pray to the Lord.
Almighty and everliving God, joy of the afflicted and strength of the suffering, hear us when we cry unto thee: in all our necessities may the presence of thy grace fill us with joy.
O Lord, hear us and have mercy.

COLLECT
The Lord be with you.
And with your spirit.
Let us pray: O merciful Lord, incline thine ear to the prayers of all who call upon thee; and that thou mayest fulfill their desires, render their requests according to thy will, through Jesus Christ, thy Son, our Lord.
Amen.

INTERCESSIONS *(Encourage people to offer their own prayers.)*

COMMON COLLECT
Almighty God, in the joy of thy presence live all the faithful departed who died in peace; we thank thee for our brothers and sisters whom thou wert pleased to deliver from the burden of the flesh and from the miseries of this world; we beseech thee soon to complete the number of thine elect, and to hasten the coming of thy kingdom, so that together with those who have fallen asleep in Christ, we may live in perfect joy of body and soul, in eternal glory, through Jesus Christ, thy Son, our Lord.
Amen.

BLESSING
Let us bless the Lord.
Thanks be to God.
May the God of all grace who called us into his eternal glory in Christ,
after our brief suffering, restore, establish, and strengthen us on a
firm foundation.
Amen.

THE HOLY EUCHARIST OR LORD'S SUPPER

*Prepare a table outside the place of worship with a number of loaves of
bread, a Bible and two lit candles. Divide the people into three groups – a
very small group, 10%, a medium, 25%, and a large, 65%. Announce
that they represent the first, second and third worlds.*

HYMN: *In Christ There Is No East or West*
In Christ there is no East or West,
    In him no South, or North;
But one great fellowship of love
    Throughout the whole wide earth.

In him shall true hearts everywhere
    Their high communion find;
His service is the golden cord
    Close binding all mankind.

Join hands, then, brothers of the faith,
    Whate'er your race may be!
Who serves My father as a son
    Is surely kin to me.

In Christ now meet both East and West,
    In him meet South and North;
All Christly souls are one in him
    Throughout the whole wide earth.
Amen.

THE DIVIDING OF THE BREAD

(Give 10% of the bread to the third world, 25% to the second world, and 65% to the first world. Ask each group to divide the bread evenly among those in their world. Remind everyone present that they live in the first world.)

RESPONSE

Alas, I am lost, I have seen the King, but my lips and my people are unclean.

Holy, holy is our God, the earth is full of his glory.

Your guilt is taken away; your sin forgiven.

Holy, holy is our God.

Whom shall I send, and who will go for us?

Here am I, send me.

Holy, holy is our God.

The earth is full of God's glory.

LITANY

Lord, you made the world and everything in it; you created the human race of one stock and gave us the earth for our caring.

Break down the walls that separate us and unite us in a single Body.

Lord, we have been divisive in our thinking, in our speech, and in our actions; we have classified and imprisoned one another; we have fenced one another out by hatred and prejudice.

Break down the walls that separate us and unite us in a single Body.

Lord, you mean us to be a single people, ruled by peace resting in freedom, freed from injustice, truly human men and women, responsible and responsive in the life we lead, the love we share, the relationships we create.

Break down the walls that separate us and unite us in a single Body.

Lord, we shall need ever-new insights into the truth, awareness of your will for all humanity, courage to do what is right even when it is not allowed, persistence in undermining unjust structures until they crumble into dust, and grace to exercise a ministry of reconciliation.

Break down the walls that separate us and unite us in a single Body.

Lord, share out among us the tongues of your Spirit, that we may

each burn with compassion for all who hunger for freedom and humanness; that we may be doers of the Word and so speak with credibility about the wonderful things you have done.
Lord, direct us in ways we do not yet discern and equip us for the service of reconciliation and liberation in your world.

SCRIPTURE *(Luke 9:10-17)*
On their return the apostles told him what they had done. And he took them and withdrew apart to a city called Bethsaida. When the crowds learned it, they followed him; and he welcomed them and spoke to them of the kingdom of God, and cured those who had need of healing. Now the day began to wear away; and the twelve came and said to him, "Send the crowd away, to go into the villages and country round about, to lodge and get provisions; for we are here in a lonely place." But he said to them, "You give them something to eat yourselves." But they said, "All we have is five loaves and two fishes, nothing more — unless perhaps we ourselves are to go and buy provisions for all this company." (There were about five thousand men.) He said to his disciples, "Make them sit down in groups of fifty or so." They did so and got them all seated. Then, taking the five loaves and the two fishes, he looked up to heaven, said the blessing over them, broke them, and gave them to the disciples to distribute to the people. They all ate to their hearts' content; and when the scraps they left were picked up, they filled twelve great baskets.

MEDITATION
(Write your own or encourage people to share their thoughts on the lesson.)

RESPONSE TO THE WORD
Let us say what we believe:
We believe in God, the Eternal Spirit, who is made known to us in Jesus Christ our brother, and to whose deeds we testify:

God calls the worlds into being,
 creates humankind in His own divine image,
 and sets before us the ways of life and death.

God seeks in holy love to save all people from aimlessness and sin.

God judges all nations and all humanity by that will of righteousness declared through prophets and apostles.

In Jesus Christ, the Man of Nazareth, our crucified and risen Lord,
    God has come to us
    and shared our common lot,
    conquering sin and death
    and reconciling the whole creation to its Creator.

God bestows upon us the Holy Spirit,
    creating and renewing the church of Jesus Christ,
    binding in covenant faithful people of all ages, tongues, and
      races.

God calls us into his church
    to accept the cost and joy of discipleship,
    to be servants in the service of the whole human family,
    to proclaim the Gospel to all the world
      and resist the powers of evil;
    to share in Christ's baptism and eat at his table;
    to join him in his passion and victory.

God promises to all who trust in the Gospel
    forgiveness of sins and fullness of grace;
    courage in the struggle for justice and peace,
    the presence of the Holy Spirit in trial and rejoicing,
    and eternal life in that kingdom which has no end.

Blessing and honor, glory and power be unto God. Amen.

INTERCESSIONS
The Lord be with you.
And with you also.
Let us pray.
**O God, your Son, Jesus Christ, taught us to pray for all persons. Let
our prayers for others be honest, asking for them those things which
they need and which you desire for them. Amen.**
Let us pray for the world:
(silent and spoken prayers)

Let us pray for our nation and those who govern it:
(silent and spoken prayers)
Let us pray for the church:
(silent and spoken prayers)
Let us pray for those in need:
(silent and spoken prayers)

Our Father in heaven:
   holy be your name,
   your kingdom come,
   your will be done,
      on earth as in heaven.
   Give us today our daily bread.
   Forgive us our sins,
      as we forgive those who sin against us.
   Save us in the time of trial,
      and deliver us from evil.
   For yours is the kingdom, the power, and the
      glory, forever. Amen.

HYMN: *Let Us Break Bread Together*
(Process from outdoors to chapel or other appropriate place of worship.)

Let us break bread together on our knees;
Let us break bread together on our knees.
When I fall on my knees, with my face to the rising sun,
O Lord, have mercy on us.

Let us drink wine together on our knees;
Let us drink wine together on our knees.
When I fall on my knees, with my face to the rising sun,
O Lord, have mercy on us.

Let us praise God together on our knees;
Let us praise God together on our knees.
When I fall on my knees, with my face to the rising sun,
O Lord, have mercy on us.

OFFERINGS

DOXOLOGY

EXCHANGE PEACE

MAKE EUCHARIST

Luke the Evangelist wrote of our risen Lord that when he was at table with two of the disciples, he took bread and blessed and broke it, and gave it to them, and their eyes were opened, and they recognized him.

In company with all believers, in every time and beyond time, we come to this table to know him in the breaking of the bread.

For the Lord Jesus, on the night he was betrayed, took bread, and, when he had given thanks, he broke it and said, "This is my Body which is broken for you. Do this in remembrance of me." In the same way also he took the cup, after supper, saying, "This cup is the new covenant in my Blood. Do this as often as you drink it, in remembrance of me."

Lift up your hearts.

We lift them to God.

Let us give thanks to God.

It is good that we do.

We give you thanks, God, Creator, Redeemer, and Sustainer, for bringing the worlds into being, for forming persons in your likeness, for recalling us when we rebel against you, and for keeping the world in your steadfast love. We praise you especially for Jesus Christ, who was born of Mary and lived as one of us; who knew exactly the life we know, and yet was obedient to your purposes, even to his death on a cross. We thank you that you stamped his death with victory by raising him in power and by making him head over all things. We rejoice in the continuing presence of the Holy Spirit, in the church you have gathered, in its task of obedience, and in the promise of eternal life. With the faithful in every place and time, we praise with joy your holy name.

Holy, holy, holy,

God of love and majesty,

The whole universe speaks of your glory,

O God, most high.

Therefore bless now, by your Word and Spirit, both us and these gifts of bread and wine, that in receiving them at this table, and in offering here our faith and praise, we may be united with Christ and one another, and remain faithful to the tasks he set before us. **In the strength Christ gives we offer ourselves to you, giving thanks that you have called us to serve you. Amen.**

BREAK THE BREAD
Through the broken bread we participate in the body of Christ.

Through the cup of blessing we participate in the new life Christ gives.

Come, for all things are ready.

EAT AND DRINK TOGETHER
The Body of Christ, broken for you.
The Blood of Christ, shed for you.
(After everyone has partaken:)
Let us give thanks.
We give thanks, almighty God, that you have refreshed us at your table by granting us the presence of your Son, Jesus Christ. Strengthen our faith, increase our love for one another, and send us forth into the world in courage and peace, rejoicing in the power of the Holy Spirit, through Jesus Christ our Lord. Amen.

HYMN: *O Jesus, I Have Promised*
O Jesus, I have promised
    To serve thee to the end;
Be thou forever near me,
    My master and my friend;
I shall not fear the battle
    If thou art by my side,
Nor wander from the pathway
    If thou wilt be my guide.

O let me hear thee speaking
    In accents clear and still,
Above the storms of passion,
    The murmurs of self-will;

O speak to reassure me,
   To hasten or control;
O speak, and make me listen,
   Thou guardian of my soul.

O Jesus, thou hast promised
   To all who follow thee
That where thou art in glory
   There shall thy servant be;
And, Jesus, I have promised
   To serve thee to the end;
O give me grace to follow,
   My master and my friend.
Amen.

BLESSING
The grace of the Lord Jesus Christ and the love of God and the
communion of the Holy Spirit, be with you all.
Amen.

*(Use the remaining bread for breakfast or spread some outside for the birds
and other of God's creatures.)*

Chapter 15

Church Life And Mission

A. Spiritual Exercise: A Conversation with the Scriptures

Direct persons to take off their shoes, sit on the floor in a circle, and make themselves very comfortable. Now ask them to close their eyes, relax, and breathe quietly. Explain to them that you are going to take them on a short journey.

Permit a minute to pass in silence, and then begin: "It is evening. All the world is quiet. You are one of a small group of Christians gathered in the upper room of a Palestinian home. You have come together to worship God. A letter has been received and you are about to hear it for the first time. It is a letter from James, the brother of Jesus, whom, you will remember, was converted by an appearance of Jesus after his resurrection. James, a servant of God and the Lord Jesus Christ and a pillar of the Christian church, has written a letter to all the churches. Be very alert. Listen carefully to his words." Then read:

> Be sure that you act on the message, and do not merely listen, for that would be to mislead yourselves. . . . My brothers and sisters, what use is it for persons to say they have faith when they do nothing to show it? Can that faith save them? Suppose a brother or sister is in rags with not enough food for the day, and one of you says, "Good luck to you, keep yourselves warm, and have plenty to eat," but does nothing to supply their bodily needs; what is the good of that? So with faith; if it does not lead to action, it is itself a lifeless thing. But someone may object: "Here is one who claims to have faith and another who points to deeds," to which I reply: "Prove to me that this faith you speak of is real though not accompanied by deeds and I by my deeds will prove you my faith." You have faith enough to believe that there is a God. Excellent! The devils have faith like that, and it makes them tremble. But can you not see, you quibbler, that faith divorced from deeds is barren?

Pause so that the group may have an opportunity to reflect on these words. Then continue: "What would you like to say to James? What do you think James would like to say to you? Visit with James for a few moments." Pause for two to three minutes. "Now it is time to close your meditation. Say farewell to James and slowly return to this place. Be silent and pray with me the prayer of St. Francis, repeating after me . . ." Give a line and let the people repeat it:

Lord, make me an instrument of your peace:
Where there is hatred, let me sow love,
where there is injury, pardon,
where there is doubt, faith,
where there is despair, hope,
where there is sadness, joy,
where there is darkness, light.
O divine Master,
    grant that I may not so much seek to be understood
    as to understand,
    not so much to be loved as to love.
For it is in giving that we receive,
    it is in pardoning that we are pardoned,
    it is in dying that we are born again to eternal life.
Amen.

Give persons an opportunity to open their eyes and return quietly. Ask if someone would like to share his or her experience. Minister to one another.

B. Educational Exercise

The aim of this session is to reflect on how your congregation has acted in the community during the past year. On newsprint, record every concrete action your congregation has taken. The list should include (1) acts of support for causes, such as money raised; (2) acts of prophetic witness, such as stands taken; (3) acts of direct service, such as "meals on wheels"; and (4) acts for systemic change, such as recall of a political figure. It can also include actions taken by single members of the congregation, provided such actions were approved and/or supported in some concrete manner by the congregation. Be as specific and as inclusive as possible. Make your list in terms of the four categories. Discuss each of these actions until everyone fully understands all of them. Include actions that failed as well as those which were successful. Strive to describe as clearly and completely as possible your congregation's life outside the church walls during the past year.

Now, review the picture just developed of your congregation's actions. How would an outsider describe your church's understanding of the meaning and purpose of the Christian life if all they knew about you were these actions?

Next, describe what the future of the world might be like if everyone behaved as you have during the past year. What vision of the world is revealed in your actions? What sort of future are you living for? Be accurate and honest.

C. Prayers

At the close of the evening have a small party, and end the session (and each of the following sessions) with evening prayers. A suggestion follows:

Let our prayers be set forth as incense, and the lifting of our hands and hearts as an evening sacrifice.

O Lord, who has pity for all our weaknesses, put away from us worry and every anxious fear, that having ended the labors of the day and committed our tasks, ourselves, and all we love into your keeping, we may now receive from you the priceless gift of peace; through Jesus Christ our Lord. Amen.

Our Father in heaven,
    hallowed be your name,
    your kingdom come,
    your will be done
        on earth as in heaven.
    Give us this day our daily bread.
    Forgive us our sins,
        as we forgive those who sin against us.
    Save us from the time of trial,
        and deliver us from evil.
    For the kingdom, the power, and the
        glory are yours now and forever. Amen.

The Lord Almighty grant us a quiet night and at the last a peaceful end and the blessing of God. Creator, Redeemer, and Sustainer, be with us all. Amen.

Exchange the Kiss of Peace.

A. Spiritual Exercise: Praying "The Jesus Prayer"

In J. D. Salinger's book *Franny and Zooey*, Franny says, "If you keep saying that prayer ["Lord Jesus Christ, Son of God, have mercy upon me"] over and over again — you only have to do it with your lips at first — then eventually . . . the prayer becomes self-active. Something happens after a while. I don't know what, but something happens and the words get synchronized with your heartbeats and then you are actually praying without ceasing." The prayer to which Franny refers is known as the "Jesus Prayer"; it dates back to the sixth century and is one of the oldest prayers in Christendom.

Have everyone sit on the floor in a circle. Play a record of plainsong or other music of the early church. After five minutes of listening and centering, suggest that everyone repeat the words of the "Jesus Prayer" together: "Lord Jesus Christ, Son of God, have mercy upon me." Direct them to close their eyes and empty their minds of all thoughts and to repeat to themselves these words over and over again. As they breathe in, they should say, "Lord Jesus Christ, Son of God," and as they exhale, "have mercy upon me." For ten minutes maintain silence as participants repeat the "Jesus Prayer" to themselves over and over again.

At the end of the time say "Amen" and then let a minute go by so that everyone can adjust to the end of the prayer. Then ask everyone to stand to hear "the Credo" from Bach's *B Minor Mass* or another appropriate piece of music.

Following the exercise, give persons an opportunity to share their experiences and minister to one another.

B. Educational Exercise: Our Understanding of the Christian Life

Give everyone time to read the following story. Encourage persons, as they read, to make those additions and corrections they believe are necessary so that this story might become their own story.

OUR STORY: ONE VERSION

In the beginning, God had a dream of a world at one with itself; it was the world God intended at creation, a world of peace and unity, of freedom and equality, of justice and the well-being of all peoples.

We were created in God's image to enjoy God's dream, but with the capacity to say "yes" or "no" to it. And so the plot thickened. We humans didn't turn out as God had hoped. We were more interested in ourselves and our own dreams than in God's dream. And so our human plight. Born with the capacity for right living, but seemingly inclined to live in estrangement from God, one another, nature, and ourselves, we continually frustrate God's dream.

But God is persistent. Having planted the dream deep within our conscience, God calls forth and raises up witnesses to the lost dream. God made a covenant with our foreparents, so that forever we will experience the unswerving, patient pull of God toward the dream. God saved us from slavery, led us on a pilgrimage to a Promised Land, and gave us moral commandments to love God and neighbors so that we might live for God's dream. God raised up leaders to guide us and at last prophets to remind us of our covenant and to sketch a picture of what the world would be like if God's dream were realized.

Still, we frustrated God's dream by acting like all the rest of humanity. It is as if we were in bondage to the social, political, and economic systems we created. So God made a decision. God acted again, came to us in Jesus of Nazareth, the dreamer, storyteller, doer of deeds, healer of hurts, advocate of the outsider, liberator of the oppressed; in Jesus God shares our common lot and overcomes the principalities and powers that keep us from living the dream.

Good news has been announced. God's dream has begun; God's dream will come. Yet the dawn of hope is not yet the high noon of God's dream come on earth. Darkness still covers much of the earth and we still live as if this were the best of all possible worlds. But a new possibility exists. We have been given a new pair of eyes and with them the vision of dreamers returns.

We have been called into a visionary community to live the risky, laughable life of tomorrow's people, to live in and for God's dream, to witness to a world of peace and unity of freedom and equality, of justice and well-being for all people. We are called to accept the cost and the joy of discipleship, to proclaim in word and deed the Good

News of God's dream come true. God promises us courage and strength in the struggle for peace and justice; God forgives us for our failures and lifts us up to new possibilities; God is present in our trials and rejoicing and hopes from this day forward.

At our baptism we were adopted into a family of dreamers called by name and given, not advantage, but the burden and responsibility of living in and for God's dream. Insofar as we live for peace and unity, freedom and equality, justice and the well-being of all people, we will be known as the children of God and the inheritors of God's promises.

Discussion
Have persons share their additions and corrections. Strive to develop a common story for your group. Then compare its understanding of the meaning and purpose of the Christian life with the meaning and purpose you discerned in your church's actions in the last session. Do you like what you see? Why and why not? What would have to be done if your pictures were to correspond? What new actions would have to be initiated if you were to live and act consistently with your understanding of the Christian story?

Have participants read the Biblical passages that follow. Suggest that each person describe concretely, in her or his own words, the world each passage envisions.

LEVITICUS 26:4-6
I will give you rain at the proper time; the land shall yield its produce and the trees of the country-side their fruit. Threshing shall last till vintage and vintage till sowing; you shall eat your fill and live secure in your land. I will give peace in the land, and you shall lie down to sleep with no one to terrify you. I will rid your land of dangerous beasts and it shall not be ravaged by war.

ISAIAH 2:4
They shall beat their swords into mattocks
    and their spears into pruning-knives;
nation shall not lift sword against nation
    nor ever again be trained for war.

ISAIAH 65:20-25

There no child shall ever again die an infant,
no old man fail to live out his life;
every boy shall live his hundred years before he dies,
whoever falls short of a hundred shall be despised.
Men shall build houses and live to inhabit them,
plant vineyards and eat their fruit;
they shall not build for others to inhabit
nor plant for others to eat.
My people shall live the long life of a tree,
and my chosen shall enjoy the fruit of their labour.
They shall not toil in vain or raise children for misfortune.
For they are the offspring of the blessed of the LORD
and their issue after them;
before they call to me, I will answer,
and while they are still speaking I will listen.
The wolf and the lamb shall feed together
and the lion shall eat straw like cattle.
They shall not hurt or destroy in all my holy mountain,
     says the Lord.

AMOS 5:24

Let justice roll on like a river
and righteousness like an ever-flowing stream.

EZEKIEL 34:25-29

I will make a covenant with them to ensure prosperity; I will rid the
land of wild beasts, and men shall live in peace of mind on the open
pastures and sleep in the woods. I will settle them in the neighborhood of my hill and send them rain in due season, blessed rain. Trees
in the country-side shall bear their fruit, the land shall yield its produce, and men shall live in peace of mind on their own soil. They
shall know that I am the LORD when I break the bars of their yokes
and rescue them from those who have enslaved them. They shall
never be ravaged by the nations again nor shall wild beasts devour
them; they shall live in peace of mind, with no one to alarm them. I
will give prosperity to their plantations; they shall never again be
victims of famine in the land nor any longer bear the taunts of the
nations.

LUKE 4:18-19

" The spirit of the Lord is upon me because he has anointed me;
he has sent me to announce good news to the poor,
to proclaim release for prisoners and recovery of sight for
   the blind;
to let the broken victims go free,
to proclaim the year of the Lord's favour."

LUKE 1:49b-55

His name is Holy;
his mercy sure from generation to generation
toward those who fear him;
the deeds his own right arm has done
disclose his might:
the arrogant of heart and mind he has put to rout,
he has brought down monarchs from their thrones,
but the humble have been lifted high.
The hungry he has satisfied with good things,
the rich sent empty away.
He has ranged himself at the side of Israel his servant;
firm in his promise to our forefathers,
he has not forgotten to show mercy to Abraham
and his children's children, for ever.

1 CORINTHIANS 12:12-26

For Christ is like a single body with its many limbs and organs,
which many as they are, together make up one body. For indeed we
were all brought into one body by baptism, in the one Spirit,
whether we are Jews or Greeks, whether slaves or free men, and that
one Holy Spirit was poured out for all of us to drink.

A body is not one single organ, but many. Suppose the foot should
say, "Because I am not a hand, I do not belong to the body," it does
belong to the body none the less. Suppose the ear were to say, "Because I am not an eye, I do not belong to the body," it does still belong
to the body. If the body were all eye, how could it hear? If the body
were all ear, how could it smell? But, in fact, God appointed each
limb and organ to its own place in the body, as he chose. If the whole
were one single organ, there would not be a body at all; in fact,
however, there are many different organs, but one body. The eye

cannot say to the hand, "I do not need you"; nor the head to the feet, "I do not need you." Quite the contrary: those organs of the body which seem to be more frail than others are indispensable, and those parts of the body which we regard as less honorable are treated with special honor. To our unseemly parts is given a more than ordinary seemliness, whereas our seemly parts need no adorning. But God has combined the various parts of the body, giving special honor to the humbler parts, so that there might be no sense of division in the body, but that all its organs might feel the same concern for one another. If one organ suffers, they all suffer together. If one flourishes, they all rejoice together.

REVELATION 21:1-5
Then I saw a new heaven and a new earth, for the first heaven and the first earth had vanished, and there was no longer any sea. I saw the holy city, new Jerusalem, coming down out of heaven from God, made ready like a bride adorned for her husband. I heard a loud voice proclaiming from the throne: "Now at last God has his dwelling among men! He will dwell among them and they shall be his people, and God himself will be with them. He will wipe every tear from their eyes; there shall be an end to death, and to mourning and crying and pain; for the old order has passed away!"

Then he who sat on the throne said, "Behold! I am making all things new!"

Discussion
Now compare the vision of God's world as found in the Scriptures with the vision revealed by your congregation's actions in the community described in the last session. Do you like what you see? How would you need to change if you were to live for God's vision?

C. Evening Prayers
End the evening by listening to "The Impossible Dream" from *Man of La Mancha* followed by evening prayers.

SESSION THREE
A. Spiritual Exercise: Matthew 5:3-10
Describe someone who seems to exemplify the qualities in each of

the following Beatitudes. Then give participants the opportunity to evaluate their own lives in terms of each quality.

Blessed are those who know their need of God;
the kingdom of heaven is theirs.
Blessed are the sorrowful; they shall find consolation.
Blessed are those of gentle spirit; they shall have
the earth as their possession.
Blessed are those who hunger and thirst
to see that justice is done; they shall be satisfied.
Blessed are those who show mercy; mercy shall be
shown them.
Blessed are those whose hearts are pure; they shall
see God.
Blessed are those who work for peace; God shall call
them his children.
Blessed are those who have suffered persecution for
the cause of right; the kingdom of heaven is theirs.

Thoughts for Reflection:

"know they need God": does not have all the answers . . . is humble
. . . dependent on God . . . is searching . . . strives to find and do
God's will.
"sorrowful": shows feelings . . . can feel with those who suffer or
hurt . . . can empathize with the outsider, the poor, the needy, the
prisoner.
"gentle spirit": affirms others . . . is concerned for people's needs
. . . has no need to prove self . . . takes the side of the unloved.
"hunger and thirst for justice": strives to see that right is done . . . is
involved in social action . . . attempts to change unjust systems
and institutions.
"show mercy": a caring person . . . sensitive to others' needs . . .
reaches out to help others . . . kind, thoughtful, and generous . . .
gives without thought of return or thanks . . . makes personal
sacrifice for public good.
"pure hearts": open and honest . . . willing to share deepest self . . .
childlike . . . free to be oneself and let others be themselves . . .
open to all others . . . wills the right and good . . . exemplary life of
religious experience and prophetic actions.

"work for peace": accepts those who are different . . . a reconciling person . . . engaged in actions to eliminate those things which prevent peace—for example, hunger, poverty, injustice, prejudice.

"suffer persecution": does what is just without worrying about the cost . . . can accept criticism . . . willing to break the law if necessary to achieve justice . . . not overly concerned about what others will think or whether one will be popular.

Close by singing "They'll Know We Are Christians by Our Love."

B. Educational Experience

Take sheets of newsprint and place them on the wall, each with a different heading, such as: Quality Education, Poverty, Hunger, Racial Justice, Healthy Environment, Sexual Equality, Peace, Economic Justice, Employment. Include as many categories as you wish. Use your understanding of God's vision for the world from the last session for ideas.

Pass out copies of newspapers and news magazines from the past month. Suggest that everyone read through them, cutting out any article that demonstrates a denial of God's desires for creation. Identify where people hurt, feel captive or oppressed, are denied power, suffer injustice, or express an unmet personal or social need. Underline a key phrase or headline in the article and then paste it under the appropriate newsprint heading.

Next, review your work and identify the two or three issues or problems that concern you most. Use the following criteria: (a) the issue has particular interest for us; (b) the issue has a clear identifiable local expression; (c) the issue is a priority concern of our denomination; (d) the issue is one we believe we can do something about.

Now break into small groups; in each group:

1. Make a list of the possible causes of the problem. For example: "Poverty—a lack of money; lack of necessities such as food, housing, and health care; lack of opportunities for employment; low wages; lack of self-esteem and motivation to work; no choices or alternatives for life-style; lack of social, economic, and political power."

2. Now identify as many local manifestations of the problem as you can. For example: "Poverty—low pay of textile workers; high rate of unemployment; inadequate housing," and so forth.
3. For each of these local manifestations describe where a person might go or what he or she might do to experience the problem firsthand. Then before the session closes have each person choose one or more of these local problems to experience alone or with someone else during the week.

Exposure Groups

Exposure experiences are opportunities to get inside an issue or problem, that is, to get a firsthand understanding. In order to understand an issue from the inside, one must see it in terms of four viewpoints:

1. From the point of view of those who are affected by the problem;
2. From the point of view of those who can do something about the problem or are involved in the problem;
3. From the point of view of those who are trying to do something about the problem; and
4. From the point of view of those who have studied the problem and are knowledgeable about it.

For example, if you are concerned about substandard housing, you first need to get a taste of what it is to live in such dwellings. To do this you can go visit and talk with the people who live there. You also need to interview the landlord who owns and rents the property, and so forth.

When you attempt to experience your problem, go with an open mind. Look and listen very carefully to everything that is going on and make an effort to hear what people are really trying to say. Put yourself in their position and be sensitive. Keep a journal of your observations and feelings as well as their comments. Ask questions. Make sure you understand. Don't try to formulate your own opinion or argue with anyone.

SESSION FOUR
A. Spiritual Exercise: Exodus 2:23-3:12

> Years passed, and the king of Egypt died, but the Israelites still groaned in slavery. They cried out, and their appeal for rescue from

their slavery rose up to God. He heard their groaning, and remembered his covenant with Abraham, Isaac and Jacob; he saw the plight of Israel, and he took heed of it.

Moses was minding the flock of his father-in-law Jethro, priest of Midian. He led the flock along the side of the wilderness and came to Horeb, the mountain of God. There the angel of the LORD appeared to him in the flame of a burning bush. Moses noticed that, although the bush was on fire, it was not being burnt up; so he said to himself, "I must go across to see this wonderful sight. Why does not the bush burn away?" When the LORD saw that Moses had turned aside to look, he called to him out of the bush, "Moses, Moses." And Moses answered, "Yes, I am here." God said, "Come no nearer; take off your sandals; the place where you are standing is holy ground." Then he said, "I am the God of your forefathers, the God of Abraham, the God of Isaac, the God of Jacob." Moses covered his face, for he was afraid to gaze on God.

The LORD said, "I have indeed seen the misery of my people in Egypt. I have heard their outcry against their slave-masters. I have taken heed of their sufferings, and have come down to rescue them from the power of Egypt, and to bring them up out of that country into a fine, broad land; it is a land flowing with milk and honey, the home of Canaanites, Hittites, Amorites, Perizzites, Hivites, and Jebusites. The outcry of the Israelites has now reached me; yes, I have seen the brutality of the Egyptians towards them. Come now; I will send you to Pharaoh and you shall bring my people Israel out of Egypt." "But who am I," Moses said to God, "that I should go to Pharaoh, and that I should bring the Israelites out of Egypt?" God answered, "I am with you. This shall be the proof that it is I who have sent you: when you have brought the people out of Egypt, you shall all worship God here on this mountain."

Now, with everyone sitting on the floor, ask them to close their eyes. Permit a minute of silence so that everyone can center in. Then explain that you are going to go together on an imaginary journey. Begin:

"You are a shepherd. The sun is just beginning to rise and you are awakening from a night's sleep. Your sheep are beginning to stir. A breeze is blowing gently and everything is at peace." Pause.

"You slowly rise and wander among the bushes and shrubs on the hillside. You can feel the ground under your feet and the warmth of the early morning. But you are startled. Before you is a bush that appears to be burning. You take off your sandals and stand staring at the bush. In the quiet you hear a voice speaking to you from out of the bush. Listen to what the voice is saying to you." Permit at least five minutes of silence.

Now softly begin to sing the first verse of "Amazing Grace"; repeat it three times:

> *Amazing grace, how sweet the sound,*
> *That saved a wretch like me!*
> *I once was lost, but now am found,*
> *Was blind, but now I see.*

End the exercise by giving persons an opportunity to share what they heard God say to them.

B. Educational Experience

Begin by giving everyone an opportunity to share an exposure-awareness experience.

Following these reports attempt to define your two or three problems or issues. For example: "Poverty—a condition of powerlessness that prevents human development of persons and groups."

Finally choose the one problem that your group would most like to address and establish a means for further investigation so that you can make an enlightened, relevant response.

The following resources for adults and youth, published by JED (Joint Educational Development) could be helpful:

1. Michael Dowling, *Health Care and the Church* (United Church Press, 1977).
2. *Maggie Kühn on Aging: A Dialogue,* edited by Dieter Hessel (Westminster Press, 1977).
3. *Metamorphosis: Christians Choosing Life-Styles for a World in Crisis* (John Knox Press, 1976).
4. Paul Minear, *I Pledge Allegiance: Patriotism and the Bible* (Westminster Press, 1975).
5. Harvey Seifert, *Good News for Rich and Poor: Christian Approaches to a New Economic Order* (United Church Press, 1977).
6. Reuben Sheares and S. Garry Oniki, *Next Steps Toward Racial Justice* (United Church Press, 1974).
7. Richard Taylor, *Economics and the Gospel* (United Church Press, 1973).

8. L. Harold de Wolf, *What Americans Should Do About Crime* (Harper & Row, 1975).

What to Do About Crime, leader's guide (United Church Press, 1977).

Beyond Survival: Bread and Justice in Christian Perspective, edited by Dieter Hessel, and *The Global Connection: Local Action for World Justice* by Dennis Shoemaker are two other suggested study books. These paperbacks are published by Friendship Press.

Chapter 16

Analysis: Social Issues

The following sessions are to be conducted using one or more of the study books suggested above.

Begin the sessions with a celebration of the Lord's Supper or Eucharist according to your tradition.

SESSION ONE:
Use the first session to meet with and talk to a person knowledgeable about the issue you've chosen, especially if you are waiting for the delivery of a study/action book.

SESSION TWO:
Plan to have another resource person, and if you have received your study/action books distribute them and suggest that the group read the first half of the book for the next session. Have one person prepare to review these chapters and lead a discussion aimed at understanding the material presented.

SESSION THREE:
During this session complete your review and discussion of the first half of the study/action book. Assign the second half of the book.

SESSION FOUR:
Complete your review and discussion of the second half of the study/action book.

SESSION FIVE:
Return the discussion to your community. Based upon your study of the problem, once again identify the local manifestations of the problem. Choose the one manifestation that you believe is most serious.

Identify what you believe is its root cause. Then ask: How do we contribute to the problem? How are we responsible for the problem? How does the problem and its cause relate to us? What can we do about it?

End the session by reviewing and preparing for the retreat.

Chapter 17

Spiritual Commitment:
A Retreat

The following retreat manual is intended to be used on a one-day retreat. It is important that you secure an isolated place where no one else is present. The plan is for persons to arrive about bed-time, settle in, and go immediately to sleep. The retreat begins at 6 A.M. and assumes a priest or minister as leader. If this is not possible, adaptations will need to be made. This retreat is to be conducted in silence except when the group is directed otherwise. Each person should be assigned a partner to act as "confessor" and guide. Further, since the group is expected to fast during the retreat, no food will be necessary. There are four segments to the retreat:

One: A Falling in Love with Jesus (6:00-9:00 A.M.)

Two: Penitence and Reconciliation (9:00-12:00 A.M.)

Three: Called to New Life (12:00-3:00 P.M.)

Four: Commitment to Christian Service (3:00-6:00 P.M.)

It is recommended that the entire congregation plan a Eucharist and fellowship supper to celebrate the group's return. Persons might individually report their commitments to the congregation in the form of an offering at the Eucharist. The aim of this retreat is to help each person become committed to new life in the world as the necessary bridge between understanding a social problem and engaging in action in the community.

ONE: *Falling in Love with Jesus*

During this three-hour segment participants will go off by themselves and read the complete Gospel According to St. Mark. There are 16 chapters. Before each chapter pray the following prayer: "Ever-present Lord, in you I live and move and have my being. I humbly pray you so to guide me by your Holy Spirit, that I may understand your Word, know you more clearly, love you more dearly, and obey you more nearly. Through Jesus Christ my Lord and Savior. Amen."

At the close of this prayer read a chapter. Meditate on your reading for five minutes, write your thoughts in a journal, and pray the prayer again. Repeat the sequence until you have completed the Gospel.

TWO: *Penitence and Reconciliation*
Gather together in one place. The following lessons from the Gospel According to St. Matthew should be read aloud, slowly and clearly: Matthew 5:1-48, 18:6-9, 25:31-46.

Team up with your partner—"confessor" and spend the next 45 minutes together. Walk in silence, meditate on the lessons, face up to your sins. Pay attention to your hidden sins or sins of omission. Toward the end of this time together confess your sins to your partner—"confessor." Remind each other of God's grace and then gather for the following liturgy.

A LITURGY OF PENITENCE
Psalm 51

Have mercy on me, O God, according to your loving-kindness;
    in your great compassion blot out my offenses.
Wash me through and through from my wickedness
    and cleanse me from my sin.
For I know my transgressions,
    and my sin is ever before me.
Against you only have I sinned
    and done what is evil in your sight.
And so you are justified when you speak
    and upright in your judgment.
Indeed, I have been wicked from my birth,
    a sinner from my mother's womb.
For behold, you look for truth deep within me
    and will make me understand wisdom secretly.
Purge me from my sin and I shall be pure;
    wash me and I shall be clean indeed.

Hide your face from my sins
  and blot out all my iniquities.
Create in me a clean heart, O God,
  and renew a right spirit within me.
Cast me not away from your presence
  and take not your holy Spirit from me.
Give me the joy of your saving help again
  and sustain me with your bountiful spirit.
Deliver me from death, O God,
  and my tongue shall sing of your righteousness,
  O God of my salvation.
The sacrifice of God is a troubled spirit;
  a broken and contrite heart, O God, you will not despise.

The Lord be with you.
And with you also.
Let us pray:
  Almighty God, you have created us out of the dust of the earth. Grant that these ashes may be to us a sign of our mortality and penitence, that we may remember that it is only by your gracious gift that we are given eternal life; through Jesus Christ our Savior. **Amen.**

(The ashes are imposed on each person's forehead by the minister or priest with the signing of the cross, saying:)
Remember __N__ that you are dust, and to dust you shall return.

(Then one at a time pray aloud the following prayer:)
I confess to Almighty God and to you, my brothers and sisters, that I have sinned through my own fault, in my thoughts and in my attitudes and in what I have done and in what I have failed to do. And I ask you, my brothers and sisters, to pray for me to the Lord our God.

Lord have mercy.
Christ have mercy.
Lord have mercy.
We have not loved you with our whole heart and mind and strength.
We have not loved our neighbors as ourselves.

Have mercy on us Lord.

We have been deaf to your call to serve as Christ served us. We have not been true to the mind of Christ. We have grieved your holy Spirit.

Have mercy on us Lord.

We confess to you, Lord, all our unfaithfulness, the pride, hypocrisy, and impatience of our lives.

Have mercy on us Lord.

Our self-indulgent appetites and ways and our exploitations of other people.

Have mercy on us Lord.

Our anger at our own frustrations and our envy of those more fortunate than we.

Have mercy on us Lord.

Our intemperate love of worldly goods and comforts and our dishonesty in daily life and work.

Have mercy on us Lord.

Our negligence in prayer and worship and our failure to commend the faith that is in us.

Have mercy on us Lord.

Our blindness to human need and suffering and our indifference to injustice.

Have mercy on us Lord.

Our uncharitable thoughts toward our neighbors and our prejudice and contempt for those who differ from us.

Have mercy on us Lord.

Our waste and pollution of your creation and our lack of concern for those who come after us.

Have mercy on us Lord.

Holy God, holy and mighty, holy immortal One, have mercy upon us. Amen.

SORROW FOR SINS

(Following this liturgy have each person go off with their partner—"confessor" and complete the following exercise:)

Read aloud Luke 18:31-43.

Privately reflect on all those things in your life that prevent you from being a faithful follower of Jesus Christ. Then identify with the blind beggar in the Gospel. Become that blind beggar. Jesus asks, "What do you want me to do for you?" Write a poem or free verse in response to Jesus' question. Express as clearly and concretely as possible all those internal psychological and external sociological factors that prevent you from being the sort of Christian in the world you believe an apostle of Jesus Christ ought to be. Then share your creation with your "confessor." Discuss your thoughts and feelings. Minister to each other.

THE RECONCILIATION OF A PENITENT
(Gather together for the following liturgy to be led by a priest or minister.)

Read Luke 15:11-32, "The Prodigal Son"; then spend five minutes in silence.
(The priest or minister begins:)
Hear the Word of God to all who truly turn to him: Come unto me all ye that travail and are heavy laden and I will refresh you. God so loved the world that he gave his only begotten Son to the end that all that believe in him should not perish but have everlasting life. This is a true saying and worthy of all persons to be received, that Christ came into the world to save sinners. Therefore in the presence of Christ and each other let us confess our sins:
(Have each person pray aloud the following prayer individually, making his or her own personal confession to God and the community. Give the community the opportunity to offer words of comfort and counsel.)
Holy God, heavenly Father, you have formed me from the dust in your image and likeness, and redeemed me from sin and death by the cross of your Son Jesus Christ. Through the water of baptism you clothed me with the shining garment of his righteousness and established me among your children in your kingdom. But I have squandered the inheritance of your saints and have wandered far in a land that is waste. Especially I confess to you and to the church . . . *(confess particular sins).* **Therefore, for these and other sins I cannot now remember, I turn to you in sorrow and repentance. Receive me again into the arms of your mercy and restore me to the blessed company of your faithful people through him in whom you have redeemed the world, your Son our Savior Jesus Christ. Amen.**

(After each person makes his or her confession and the community offers comfort and counsel the minister or priest says to the penitent:)
Will you turn again to Christ our Lord?
I will.
Do you forgive those who have sinned against you?
I forgive them.
May Almighty God in mercy receive your confession of sorrow and of faith, strengthen you in all goodness and by the power of the Holy Spirit keep you in eternal life. **Amen.**
(The minister or priest then lays hands on each penitent's head and says:)
Almighty God have mercy on you, forgive you all your sins through Jesus Christ our Lord, strengthen you in all goodness and by the power of the Holy Spirit keep you in eternal life. **Amen.**

(After everyone has confessed their individual sins, the community should pray together:)
Most merciful God, we also confess that we have corporately sinned against you in thought, word, and deed by what we as a church have done and by what we have left undone. We are truly sorry and we humbly repent. For the sake of your Son Jesus Christ have mercy upon your church and forgive us of our sins that we may delight in your will and walk in your way, to the glory of your name. Amen.

Almighty God have mercy on us, forgive us all our sins, strengthen the church in all goodness, and by the power of the Holy Spirit keep us in eternal life. **Amen.**
Now there is rejoicing in heaven; for we are lost and are found; we were dead and are now alive in Christ our Lord. Let us go in peace. The Lord has put away all our sins.
Thanks be to God.
Exchange the peace.

THREE: *Called to Newness of Life*
The next series of exercises are to be used by pairs of partner-"confessors." After each exercise pray:
Take, O Lord, all my freedom. Receive my feelings, my understandings and my will. You have given me all that I am and all that I possess. I return it to you and surrender it to the guidance of your

will. Give me only your love and grace. With these I am rich enough and ask nothing more. Amen.

A. PETER'S DECLARATION

Read Mark 8:27-38.

Jesus asks you, "Who do you say that I am?" Explain to each other the difference Jesus makes in your life.

Jesus explains that anyone who wishes to be a disciple must leave self behind, take up his cross, and follow after; state concretely what you believe this means for you in the months ahead.

B. JESUS AND ZACCHAEUS

Read Luke 19:1-10.

Zacchaeus, after his conversion, made some significant changes in his life. Explain to each other what changes you intend to make in your lives in the months ahead.

C. THE GREAT COMMAND

Read Matthew 22:34-40.

Explain how you think you can best demonstrate your love of God and your love of all who are in any need? What concrete actions do you intend to take in the months ahead that will prove your love?

D. JESUS AND PETER

Read John 21:15-19.

Explain where it is that Jesus is leading you; that is, where you don't want to go and what you don't want to do that will witness to the Gospel's good news for all those who know only the bad news of injustice, poverty, hunger, and other adversity.

E. A VISION

Read Acts 11:1-17.

Explain, if you had a similar vision, what you would see in the sailcloth. Explain what you need to do in the light of that vision. Be specific.

F. GOD IS LOVE

Read 1 John 4:7-21.

Explain concretely what you need to do if you are to live so that the unloved will experience the love of God through you.

FOUR: *Commitment To Christian Service.*
(The following is a final liturgy:)

What are we by nature?
We are part of God's creation made in the image of God.
What does it mean to be created in the image of God?
It means that we are free to make choices, to love, to create, to reason, and to live in harmony with creation and with God.
What is meant by a covenant with God?
A covenant is a relationship initiated by God to which a body of people responds in faith.
What is the church?
The church is the community of the New Covenant.
What is the New Covenant?
The New Covenant is the new relationship with God given by Jesus Christ the Messiah to the apostles and to all who believe in him.
How is the church described in the Bible?
The church is described as the body of which Christ is the head and of which all baptized persons are members. It is called the people of God, a holy nation, a royal priesthood.
What is the mission of the church?
The mission of the church is to restore all people to unity with God and each other in Christ.
How does the church pursue its mission?
The church pursues its mission as it prays and worships, proclaims the Gospel, and promotes justice, peace, and love.
Through whom does the church carry out its mission?
The church carries out its mission through the ministry of all its members.
What is the Christian hope?
The Christian hope is to live with confidence in newness and full-ness of life and to await the coming of Christ in glory and the completion of God's purposes for the world.
What is prayer?
Prayer is responding to God through word and deed.

What prayer did Christ teach us?
Our Lord taught us to say:
    Our Father in Heaven:
    hallowed be your name,
    your kingdom come,
    your will be done,
    on earth as in heaven.
Give us today our daily bread.
Forgive us our sins,
    As we forgive those
    who sin against us.
Save us in the time of trial,
    And deliver us from evil.
For the kingdom, the power,
    and the glory are yours,
    now and forever. Amen.

LESSONS
Read Matthew 25:14-46.
(Give each person an opportunity to describe his or her talents, gifts, blessings, and specifically how he or she might use them in gratitude to God and on behalf of his or her neighbor in need.)
Read Luke 6:43-45.
(Give each person an opportunity to explain what God is calling him or her to be and do. After each statement, the minister or priest asks:)
And do you commit yourself to this Christian service?
I do, Christ being my helper.
(The minister or priest puts his or her hands on the person's head and prays:)
Almighty God, look with favor upon   N   who has now reaffirmed commitment to follow Christ and serve in his name. Give him/her courage, patience, and vision, and strengthen us all in our Christian vocation of witness to the world and service to others through Jesus Christ our Lord. Amen.
(After the last person has been commissioned, say:)
Let us pray for the church and the world: For the mission of the church that through faithful action it may witness to the Gospel to the ends of the earth, we pray to you, O Lord:
(intercessions)

Almighty God, who created us in your own image: Grant us grace that we may fearlessly contend against evil and take no peace with oppression. May we reverently use our freedom, and help us to employ it in the quest for justice in our communities and among all peoples to the glory of your holy name, through Jesus Christ Our Lord who lives and reigns with you and the Holy Spirit, one God now and forever. Amen.

May the God of hope fill us with all joy and peace in believing through the power of the Holy Spirit. **Amen.**

Let us go forth into the world rejoicing in the power of the Spirit. **Thanks be to God.**

Chapter 18

Community Action

The next four weeks are divided into two sections: Learning to Engage in Social Action and Planning to Act. Read the following outline and plan the next sessions carefully. It is important that you have the necessary copies of the resource book to pass out, and that participants are committed to the reading and preparation necessary for each week's two-hour session.

Before each session use the following or another appropriate prayer: Almighty God, the fountain of all wisdom: Enlighten by your Holy Spirit our learning, that, rejoicing in the knowledge of your truth, we may worship you and serve you all the day long; through Jesus Christ our Lord, who lives and reigns with you and the Holy Spirit, one God forever and ever. Amen.

At the close of the session use the following or other appropriate prayers:

The Lord be with you.

And with your spirit.

Let us pray:

I ask your prayers for all God's people throughout the world; for this gathering; and for all ministers, lay and ordained. Pray for the church . . . (*Silence. People offer prayers.*)

I ask your prayers for peace; for goodwill among nations; and for the well-being of all people. Pray for justice and peace . . . (*Silence and prayers.*)

I ask your prayers for the poor, the hungry, the sick, the oppressed, and those in prison. Pray for those in any need or trouble . . . (*Silence and prayers.*)

I ask your prayers for all who seek God or a deeper knowledge of him. Pray that they may find and be found by him . . . (*Silence and prayers.*)

I ask your prayers for the departed. Pray for those who have died
. . . *(Silence and prayers.)*

Praise God for those in every generation who have witnessed to
the Gospel. Pray that we may have grace to act with Christ in our own
day . . . *(Silence and prayers.)*

Hasten O Lord the coming of your kingdom and grant that we your
servants, who now live by faith, may do your will, through Jesus
Christ our Lord. **Amen.**

SECTION ONE: Learning to Engage in Social Action

SESSION ONE

Essential to the next three sessions is the paperback book *A Social
Action Primer* by Dieter Hessel (Westminster Press). Each person in
your group will need one of these books.

In preparation for this first session, read chapter 2, "What Is Social
Action?"; chapter 3, "Some Related Activities"; and chapter 4, "Radical End, Realistic Means." When you gather, discuss these three
chapters.

1. Do you agree with the author's definition of social action? Why or
   why not? How would you revise it?
2. Using the author's definition, identify the times when your congregation has been involved in social action. When has your denomination been involved in social action?
3. Consider all the related activities identified by the author and
   make a list of the occasions when your congregation has been
   engaged in each. Which of these activities do you feel most comfortable with? Which are most acceptable to your congregation?
4. In chapter 3 of *A Social Action Primer*, the author notes the difference between social education, social service, social witness, and
   social action. Briefly characterize the emphasis of each type of
   social involvement in preparation for listing your group's in-
   volvements.

On newsprint, list activities of each type that involve your
group. Include both activities that are initiated and those that are
supported by members of your group. Typically churches and the
organizations to which they relate are more involved in education
and service than they are in public affairs witness or action in-

tended to change social structures. The session might conclude with discussion of the reasons for this disparity.

5. Turn to page 125 in *A Social Action Primer*—the appendix. Examine the social involvement styles presented and identify which seems best for you. Explain why!

6. To what radical ends can you commit yourself? What realistic means can you accept?

7. What needs to happen to you, your group, your church so that you may become a realistic radical? What can be done to make that happen?

8. Review what you have learned.

SESSION TWO

In preparation for this session read chapter 5, "Strategic Thinking," in *A Social Action Primer*. Thinking strategically is a skill the author wants all his readers to develop, so he organizes the subject around five easy-to-remember questions (page 68.) Begin by choosing any social problem facing your community. Then attempt to answer the five strategy questions. The exposition of each question can be looked at both in terms of a checklist of things to consider and as a tool kit. Note especially the following tools for strategic thinking in relation to: question 1, page 75; question 2, pages 80-82; question 3, pages 83-88; question 4, pages 91-93, 101-102; and question 5, pages 107-108. Your aim is to practice strategic thinking. The problem you choose is not as important as being able to answer the questions.

The leader(s) of this session should attempt to apply this method of strategic thinking to the actual social involvement planning of the group. Your discussion can help to identify aspects of previous planning that were inadequate. For example: Whom did you consult in defining a social problem or project? What kinds of power did you seek to exercise or put into motion? Did you approach the action goal in terms of concrete operational steps? What tactics did you consider and then emphasize? What action outcome did you expect and get?

If you have time, choose a second problem and go through the questions again. Review what you have learned.

SESSION THREE

In preparation for this session read chapter 6, "Analyzing Tactics," in *A Social Action Primer*.

1. Discuss each of the tactics presented in this chapter. What do you believe are the advantages and disadvantages of each? As you consider social problems in your community and who you are, which tactic(s) do you consider most relevant?
2. Attempt to conceive of other strategies not mentioned. Brainstorm possibilities. Do not ask if they are possible or reasonable. See if you can discover new ways to effect change in the world.
3. Practice. Take a social problem and strive to agree on a tactic to address it. Use the guidelines presented in this chapter. If you are successful and have time, do the same with a second problem.
4. Review what you have learned.

SECTION TWO: Planning To Act

SESSION FOUR
Together complete the following planning guide.

Step One: Problem Definition
Local social issue chosen to be addressed:

Problem description (write a statement of the problem as you understand it):

Goals (What do you hope to accomplish by your action?):

Step Two: Analysis and Clarification
Problem Analysis
What is the cause of the problem?

How does the problem and its cause relate to you?

Who is affected by this problem and how do they perceive it?

Who will be in favor of change? How will they show it?

Who will be opposed to any change? How will they show it?

What other groups in the community are concerned about the problem? How are they working on it? How can you cooperate?

What additional information do you need about the issue before you can proceed?

Clarification of Goal
Do you fully understand your goal? What exactly are you trying to do?

Is your goal realistic? Timely?

Do you have the skills and resources to achieve your goal? Can you do it alone or do we need others? Who?

Step Three: Review of Alternatives
Alternative Strategies
List the possible concrete actions you might take and their consequences:

Action	Consequences	
	Desirable	Undesirable

From this list of alternatives, determine a tentative plan for action:

Evaluate your action plan:
　Are you committed to this action?

　Is it possible and realistic?

　Will this action help you meet your goal?

Step Four: Communication and Involvement
Relevant Groups
What other groups and individuals need to be involved and what is the best way to involve them?

Individuals and groups   Type of involvement

How and when will you communicate your plan to them?

How will others respond to your action strategy?

Does your goal or action plan need to be redefined or modified? Why? How?

Step Five: Action
Procedure
List the steps in your action plan, who is responsible, and a timetable for its completion.

Action   Responsibility   Completion Date

Do these assigned responsibilities make the best use of resources and abilities?

How and when will progress and problems be assessed?

How can the action strategy be modified, if necessary?

Now it is time to act.

Step Six: Reflection and Follow-Up
Outcomes
What happened?

Positive results   Negative results

Will the program be continued? With modifications? By whom?

What future outcomes can be anticipated?

Follow-Up

What new concerns, issues, problems were identified?

What next steps should be taken?

What lessons about social issues and social action strategies may be drawn from your experience?

And so we come to the close of this learning design. If it has been successful, you should have had some experience of God, you should have had your faith enhanced and enlivened, and you should have gained both a greater sense of your vocation in the world and some skills for responsible Christian action. I would hope that your devotional life of piety toward God has been enriched and your prophetic life of action on behalf of those denied God's will has been empowered. Further, I trust that your faith in God's Word has been renewed, your daily life has been made more meaningful and purposeful, and your vision of God's future has been clarified.

More important, I hope that you have gained an awareness of your learning needs and a sense of how you might best proceed in your pilgrimage of faith and life as a believer in Jesus Christ and a member of his Church.

If you have made some new beginnings and commitments; if you have acquired a greater sense of piety through inner growth and a corresponding sense of prophetic power for outer change, then this small effort at encouraging personal, church, and societal renewal and reform has been realized. Since you began, more than three months have passed. A great many hours have been committed to study, prayer, and activity. You are now ready and, I hope, stimulated to engage together in reponsible social action in your community. May it prove to be a faihful attempt to do the Word. Through it may you continue to grow and your community change that the Gospel may be communicated through word and deed to all the world. Now go forth to love and serve the Lord. Thanks be to God. Amen.

Epilogue:

JUDGING FAITHFULNESS

Below are a number of criteria that can be used to evaluate congregational life. Reflect on each one and establish how well they have been met. Use your evaluation both to judge your efforts at reform and renewal and to initiate new efforts toward those ends.

1. Our adults possess a personal knowledge and understanding of God's revelation as found in Scriptures, and they are both disposed and able to interpret its meaning for daily social life.

    Proof: Our adults are engaged in reflection on social issues in the light of the Christian faith.

    Our adults are engaged in efforts to reform the life of the church in the world so that it might be responsive and responsible to the Gospel.

2. Our adults are committed to Jesus Christ as Lord and Savior and are faithfully and responsibly responding to Christ's call to mission and ministry.

    Proof: Our adults are meaningfully engaged in acts of both piety and prophetic action.

    Our adults live in the community in ways that demonstrate the transforming power of the Gospel.

3. Our adults are committed to the radical demands of Christian vocation in the world.

    Proof: Our adults make their moral decisions and act faithfully and responsibly in their daily individual and corporate lives to the ends that God's will is done and God's community comes.

4. Our adults are committed to the church's corporate mission in the world for justice, liberation, whole community, peace, and the well-being of all persons.

    Proof: Our adults are engaged in concrete corporate social actions aimed at the transformation of the world.